Privilege, Power, and Difference

Allan G. Johnson

*Hartford College for Women
of the University of Hartford*

Boston   Burr Ridge, IL   Dubuque, IA   Madison, WI   New York
San Francisco   St. Louis   Bangkok   Bogotá   Caracas   Kuala Lumpur
Lisbon   London   Madrid   Mexico City   Milan   Montreal   New Delhi
Santiago   Seoul   Singapore   Sydney   Taipei   Toronto

McGraw-Hill Higher Education

A Division of The *McGraw-Hill* Companies

PRIVILEGE, POWER, AND DIFFERENCE

Published by McGraw-Hill, an imprint of The McGraw-Hill Companies, Inc. 1221 Avenue of the Americas, New York, NY 10020. Copyright © 2001 by The McGraw-Hill Companies, Inc. All rights reserved. No part of this publication may be reproduced or distributed in any form or by any means, or stored in a database or retrieval system, without the prior written consent of The McGraw-Hill Companies, Inc., including, but not limited to, in any network or other electronic storage or transmission, or broadcast for distance learning. Some ancillaries, including electronic and print components, may not be available to customers outside the United States.

4 5 6 7 8 9 0 BAN/BAN 0 9 8 7 6 5 4 3 2

ISBN 0-7674-2254-6

Allan Johnson is a frequent speaker on college and university campuses. If you would like to arrange an event at your school, you can reach him at (860) 768-5605 or by email at agjohnson@mail.hartford.edu. For more on his work, visit his web site at http://uhavax.hartford.edu/genderknot.

Sponsoring editor, Serina Beauparlant; production editor, Julianna Scott Fein; manuscript editor, Anne Montague; design manager, Violeta Diaz; text designer, Linda Robertson; cover designer, Joan Greenfield; art editor and illustrator, Robin Mouat; manufacturing manager, Randy Hurst. The text was set in 10.5/14 New Baskerville by TBH Typecast, Inc., and printed on acid-free 50# Butte des Morts by Banta Book Group.

Credits: Chapter 10 is excerpted and adapted from the chapter entitled "Unraveling the Gender Knot," included in *The Gender Knot: Unraveling Our Patriarchal Legacy*, by permission of Temple University Press. Copyright © 1997 by Allan G. Johnson. All rights reserved; page 151, from *Hands Laid upon the Wind*, by Bonaro Overstreet. Copyright © 1955 by W. W. Norton, Inc. By permission of W. W. Norton, Inc.

Library of Congress Cataloging-in-Publication Data
Johnson, Allan G.
    Privilege, power, and difference / Allan G. Johnson.
      p. cm.
    Includes bibliographical references and index.
    ISBN 0-7674-2254-6
    1. Elite (Social sciences)—United States. 2. Power (Social sciences)—United States. 3. Social conflict—United States. I. Title
HN90.E4 J64 2000
303.3—dc21   00-058673

www.mhhe.com

Contents

For Jane Tuohy

Introduction

I wrote this little book for one reason. We all know that a great deal of trouble surrounds issues of difference in this society, trouble relating to gender and race, sexual orientation, ethnicity, social class. A huge store of knowledge, from scientific research to passionate memoirs, documents this trouble and leaves no doubt that it causes enormous amounts of injustice and unnecessary suffering.

For all that we know, however, we still don't seem to have an understanding of the trouble we're in that allows us to do something about it. We are, both individually and collectively, stuck in a kind of paralysis that perpetuates the trouble and its human consequences.

All of us are part of the problem. There is no way to avoid that as long as we live in the world. But we could also make ourselves part of the solution if only we knew how. This book provides a way of thinking about the trouble that has the potential to help us become part of the solution by getting us unstuck. It provides a framework that is conceptual and theoretical on the one hand and grounded in the experience of everyday life on the other. Thus it allows us to see not only where the trouble comes from, but how we as individuals are connected to it, which is the only thing that gives us the potential to make a difference.

When most people read the phrase "how we as individuals are connected to it," they think they're about to be told they've done something wrong, that blame and guilt aren't far behind, especially if they are white or male or heterosexual or of a privileged class. This defensive reaction has done more than perhaps anything else to keep us stuck in our current paralysis by preventing each of us from taking the steps required to become part of the solution.

As a white, male, heterosexual, middle-class professional, I know about such feelings from my own life. But as a sociologist, I also know that it's possible to understand the world and myself in relation to it in ways that get past the defensive feelings and give us all a common ground from which to work for change. My purpose in this book is to articulate that understanding in ways that are clear and compelling and, above all, useful. The sociological framework the book offers is conceptual and theoretical. It is about how we think. But always the purpose is to change how we think so that we can change how we act, and by changing how we participate in the world, become part of the complex dynamic through which the world itself will change.

Because my primary goal is to change how people think about issues of difference and privilege, I've been less concerned with describing all the forms that difference can take and the problems associated with them. In choosing, I've been drawn to forms of difference that are the most pervasive, that affect the greatest number of people, and that produce the most harm. Also, like any author, I tend to stick to what I know best. As a result, I focus almost entirely on gender, race, social class, and, in a less extensive way, sexual orientation.

Because the nature of class is unique, I don't analyze it in the same way that I look at other forms of difference. Class differences have huge effects on people's lives, but class is fundamentally different from gender, race, and sexual orientation. The most important difference is that while we all have the potential to change our class position, the other forms of difference are almost impossible to change. Unlike class, differences of gender, race, and sexual orientation are associated with the body itself. From the moment of birth, for example, the assignment of people to categories of female or male is based almost entirely on their physical attributes and appearance.

But class still figures prominently in the book, because class differences and the capitalist economic system that produces them play a key role in how the trouble around difference works and how each of us experiences it. The historical roots of modern racism, for example, are primarily economic, and while racism is a problem that involves all white people, how it plays out in white people's lives varies depending on their social class. In some ways, for example, the social advantage of being white will tend to be more significant for lower- and working-class whites than it will for whites in the middle and upper classes. A lack of class privilege can make it more important to draw upon white privilege as a form of compensation. Without taking such patterns into account, it's difficult to know just what something like "race privilege" means.

To some degree, this book cannot help having a white, straight, male, middle-class point of view, because that's what my background is. But that combination of social characteristics does not simply limit me, for each also provides a bridge from my own experience to some portion of almost every reader's life. I cannot know from my own experience, for example, what it's like to be a woman or a person of color or a homosexual in this society. But I can bring my experience as a white person to the struggle of white people—including white women and lower-class white men—to deal with the subject of racism, just as I can bring my experience as a man to men's work—including gay men and men of color—around the subject of sexism and male privilege. In the same way, I can bring my experience as a straight person to the challenge faced by heterosexuals—of whatever gender or race or class—who want to come to terms with heterosexism and homophobia.

What I don't know from my own experience I have to supplement by studying the experience and research and writings of others, which I've been working at since I received my Ph.D. in sociology almost thirty years ago. During that time, I've designed and taught courses on class and capitalism, the sociology of gender, feminist theory, and, with a female African American colleague, race in the United States. I've written a book on gender inequality (*The Gender Knot: Unraveling Our Patriarchal Legacy*). I've been active in the movement against violence against women and have done diversity training in corporations and universities.

None of this means I'm in a position to say the last word on anything or that this book will reflect everyone's experience of difference and privilege. If, however, I've succeeded in what I set out to do here—and only you will know if I have—then I believe the result will be a book that has something to offer almost everyone who wants to deal with these difficult issues and help change the world for the better.

Allan G. Johnson
Collinsville, Connecticut

CHAPTER 1

Rodney King's Question

In 1991, a black motorist named Rodney King suffered a brutal beating at the hands of police officers in Los Angeles. When his assailants were acquitted—in spite of evidence that included a videotape of the incident—and riots broke out in Los Angeles, King uttered the exasperated plea that would become famous as it echoed across the long history and deep divide of racism in the United States. "Can't we all just get along?"

His words formed a simple yet eloquent summary of the current state of our racial dilemma, what the black leader and scholar W. E. B. Du Bois called a century ago "the problem of the color line." But in King's few words, he said more than that. Past his exasperation lies a real and serious question, one that has haunted us ever since the Civil War brought down the institution of slavery. Like any serious question, it sits and waits for what it deserves, which is a serious answer.

At the dawn of the twenty-first century, it is clear that however much people might wish it otherwise, the answer is still no.

Whether it's a matter of can't or won't, the truth is that we simply don't get along. Segregation in housing and schools is stubborn and pervasive, and the average wealth of white families is almost ten times that of blacks. The steady corrosion that everyday racism causes to the fabric of social life is everywhere. It especially galls middle-class blacks who believed what whites told them, that if they did everything right—if they went to school and worked hard and made something of themselves—race would no longer be an issue. But they soon discovered, and they learn anew every day, that nothing seems to protect them from their vulnerability to white racism.

As I write this, I'm aware that some readers—whites in particular, and especially those who don't have the luxury of class privilege—may already feel put off by my use of words like *racism, white,* and, even worse, *white racism.* One way to avoid such reactions is to follow the advice I was once given to not use the words at all. As the rest of this book will try to make clear, however, if we dispense with the words we make it impossible to talk about what's really going on and what it has to do with us. And if we can't do that, then we can't see what the problems are or how we might make ourselves part of the solution to them, which is, after all, the only worthwhile point of writing or reading a book such as this one.

With that in mind, perhaps the most important thing I can say to reassure readers who are wondering whether to continue is that things are not what they seem. The defensive and irritable feelings that whites often experience when they come across such language are based on some fundamental misperceptions of the world which this book will try to clarify and set straight. If I succeed at that, then the meaning and emotional weight of concepts like "privilege" and "white racism" will soften and shift.

Problems of perception and defensiveness apply not only to the language of race, but to an entire set of social differences that have become the basis for a great deal of trouble in the world. Although Du Bois was correct that color would be a defining issue in the twentieth century, the problem of "getting along" doesn't stop there. It is also an issue across differences of gender, sexual orientation, and numerous lesser divides. Men's violence and harassment aimed at women is epidemic in the United States, for example, and show no sign of letting up anytime soon. The glass ceiling that lets women see the executive suite but keeps them from being promoted to it is as thick as ever, and the gender gap in income is narrowing only at a glacial pace and persists even among top executives in Fortune 500 companies. Men dominate virtually every major organization and institution, from corporations to government to organized sport and religion, and for all the hype about the "new father," men rarely feel as responsible for domestic work and child care as their female partners do. Harassment and discrimination directed at gay men and lesbians are commonplace, and although physical violence and murder are more rare, they are an ever-present reminder of the dangers of being identified as anything other than heterosexual.

Clearly, we aren't getting along with one another, and we need to ask why not.

For many, the answer is some variation on "human nature." People can't help fearing the unfamiliar—including people of other races, goes one popular argument. Or women and men are so dissimilar it's as though they they come from separate planets, and it's some kind of cross-cultural (if not cross-species) miracle that we get along as well as we do. Or there is only one natural sexual orientation (heterosexual), and all the rest are therefore unacceptable and bound to cause conflict wherever they become obvious. Or those who are more capable will get more than everyone else—they always have and they always will. Someone, after all, has to be on top.

As popular and powerful as such arguments are, the only way to hold on to them is to ignore most of what history, psychology, anthropology, sociology, biology, and, if people look closely, their own experience reveal about human beings and how they live. We are not prisoners to some natural order that pits us hopelessly and endlessly against one another. We are prisoners to *something,* but it's closer to our own making than we realize. And we, therefore, are far from helpless to change it and ourselves.

CHAPTER 2

We're In Trouble

Every morning before breakfast I walk with our dogs, Sophie and Elsie, in acres of woods behind our house in the northwest hills of Connecticut. It's a quiet and peaceful place. I can feel the seasons come and go. Winter lies long and deep beneath one snowfall layered on another. Come spring, fiddlehead ferns uncoil from the forest floor and then summer exhausts itself before sliding into the cool, crisp clarity of autumn.

I like the walks mostly for the solitude. I can reflect on my life and the world and see things in perspective and more clearly. And I like to watch the dogs crash through the woods as they chase each other in games of tag, sniff out fresh deer scat or the trail of an animal that passed through the night before. They go out far and then come back to make sure I'm still there.

It's hard not to notice that everything seems pretty simple to them—or at least from what I can see. They never stray far from what I imagine to be their essence, the core of what it means to be a dog in relation to everything around them, living and otherwise. And that's all they seem to need or care about.

It's also hard not to wonder about my own species, which, by comparison, is deeply troubled most of the time. I suspect we don't have to be, because even though I'm trained as a sociologist to see the complexity of things, it seems to me that we're also fairly simple. Deep in our bones, for example, we are social beings. There's no escaping it. We can't survive on our own when we're young, and it doesn't get a whole lot easier later on. We need to feel that we belong to something bigger than ourselves, whether it's a family or a team or a society. We look to other people to tell us that we measure up, that we matter, that we're okay. We have a huge capacity to be creative and generous and loving. We spin stories, make art and music, help children turn into adults, save one another in countless ways, and ease our loved ones into death when the time comes. We have large brains and opposable thumbs and are incredibly clever in how we use them. I'm not sure if we're the only species with a sense of humor—I think I've seen dogs laugh—but we've certainly made the most of it. And we're astonishingly adaptable. We can figure out how to live just about anywhere under almost any conditions you could imagine. We can take in the strange and unfamiliar and learn to understand and embrace it, whether it's a new language or an odd food or the mysteries of death and dying or the person sitting next to us on the crosstown bus who doesn't look like anyone we've seen before.

For all our potential, you'd think we could manage to get along with one another. By that I don't mean love one another in some profoundly idealistic way. We don't need to love one another—or even *like* one another—to work together or just share space in the world. I also don't mean something as minimal as mere tolerance or refraining from overt violence. I mean that you'd think we could treat one another with decency and respect and appreciate if not support the best we have in us. It's what I imagine Rodney King meant by "get along."

It doesn't seem unreasonable to imagine a school or a workplace, for example, where all kinds of people feel comfortable showing up, secure in the knowledge that they have a place they don't have to defend every time they turn around, where they're encouraged to do their best, and valued for it. We all like to feel that way: accepted, valued, supported, appreciated, respected, belonging. So you'd think we'd go after it like dogs on the scent of something good to eat. We'd go after it, that is, unless something powerful kept us from it.

Apparently, something powerful does keep us from it, to judge from all the trouble there is around issues of difference—especially in relation to race, gender, sexual orientation, and class. Something powerful keeps us far from anything like a world where people feel comfortable showing up and feel good about themselves and one another. The truth of this powerful force is everywhere, but we don't know how to talk about it, and so we act as though it's always somewhere other than here and now in the room with us.

A few years ago I was sitting across a restaurant table from an African American woman. We were talking about a course on race and gender that we wanted to teach together. And while we talked about what we wanted our students to think about and learn, I felt how hard it was for me to talk about race and gender in that moment—about how the legacy of racism and sexism shapes our lives in such different ways, how my whiteness and maleness are sources of privilege (another of those words that can get people going) that elevates me not above some abstract groups, but above her, my friend.

The simple truth is that when I go shopping, I'll probably get waited on faster and better than she will. I'll benefit from the cultural assumption that I'm a serious customer who doesn't need to be followed around to keep me from stealing something. The clerk won't ask me for three kinds of ID before accepting my check or accepting my credit card. But all these indignities that my whiteness protects me from are part of her everyday existence. And it doesn't matter how she dresses or behaves or that she's an executive in a large corporation. Her being black and the realtors' and bankers' and clerks' being white in a racist society is all it takes.

She also can't go for a walk alone at night without thinking about her safety a lot more than I would—without planning what to do in case a man approaches her with something other than good will. She has to worry about what a man might think if she smiles in a friendly way and says hello as they pass on the sidewalk, or what he'll think if she doesn't. She has to decide where to park her car for the greatest safety, to remember to have her keys out and ready as she approaches it, and to check the back seat before she gets in. In other words, she has to draw a tight boundary around her life in ways that never occur to me, and her being female is the only reason why.

As these thoughts filled my mind, I struggled with how to sit across from her and talk and eat our lunch while all of this is going on all the time. I wanted to say, "Can we talk about this and *us*?" But I didn't, because it felt risky, the kind of thing you both know but keep at bay by not actually *saying* it, like a married couple where one's been unfaithful and both know it but collude in silence to keep the thing going. They realize that if either speaks the truth they both already know, they won't be able to go on as if this gulf and hurt between them weren't there.

It's not that I've *done* something or thought bad thoughts or harbored ill will toward her because she's black and female. No, the problem is that in the world as it is, huge issues involving race and gender shape her life and mine in dramatically different ways. And it's not some random accident that befell her while I escaped. A tornado didn't blow through town and level her house while leaving mine alone. No, her misfortune is connected to my fortune; the reality of her having to deal with racism and sexism every day is connected to the reality that I *don't*. I didn't have to do anything wrong for this to be true and neither did she. But there it is just the same.

All of that sits in the middle of the table like the proverbial elephant that everyone pretends not to notice.

The "elephant" is a society and its people for whom a decent and productive social life that is true to the best of our essential humanity continues to be elusive. In its place is a powerful kind of trouble that is tenacious, profound, and seems only to get worse. I can't help wondering how much worse it will get.

The trouble we're in privileges some groups at the expense of others. It creates a yawning divide in levels of income, wealth, dignity, safety, health, and quality of life. It promotes fear, suspicion, discrimination, harassment, and violence. It sets people against one another. It builds walls topped with broken glass and barbed wire. It weaves the insidious and corroding effects of oppression into the daily lives of tens of millions of women, men, and children. It has the potential to ruin entire generations and, in the long run, to take just about everyone down with it.

It is a trouble that shows up everywhere and touches every life in one way or another. There is no escape, however thick the denial. It's in families and neighborhoods, in schools and churches, in government and the courts, and especially in colleges and the workplace, where many people have their first true experience with people unlike themselves and what this society makes of such differences.

The hard and simple truth is that the "we" that's in trouble is all of us—not just straight white middle- and upper-class males—and it will take all or at least most of us to get us out of it. It's relatively easy, for example, for white people to fall into the safe and comfortable rut of thinking that racism is a problem that belongs to people of color, or for men to see sexism as a women's issue, or for members of the middle and upper classes to see poverty as people's own fault. But such thinking mistakes fantasy for reality. It pretends we can talk about "up" without "down" or that a "you" or a "them" can mean something without a "me" or an "us." There is no way that a problem of difference can involve just one group of people. The "problem" of race can't be just a problem of being black, Chinese, Sioux, or Mexican. It has to be more than that, because there is no way to separate the "problem" of being, say, black from the "problem" of *not* being white. And there is no way to separate the problem of not being white from *being* white. This means privilege is always a problem for people who don't have it and for people who do, because privilege is *always* in relation to others. Privilege is always at someone else's expense and always exacts a cost. Everything that's done to receive or maintain it—however passive and unconscious—results in suffering and deprivation for someone.

We live in a society that attaches privilege to being white and male and heterosexual regardless of your social class. If I don't see how that makes me part of the problem of privilege, I won't see myself as part of the solution. And if people in privileged groups don't include themselves in the solution, the default is to leave it to blacks and women and Asians, Latinos, Native Americans, lesbians, gay men, and the lower and working classes to do it on their own. But these groups can't do it on their own, because they don't have the power to change entrenched systems of privilege by themselves. If they could do that, there wouldn't be a problem in the first place.

The simple truth is that the trouble we're in can't be solved unless people who are heterosexual or male or Anglo or white or economically comfortable feel obligated to make the problem of privilege *their* problem and to do something about it. For myself, it means I have to take the initiative to find out how privilege operates in the world, how it affects people, and what all that has to do with me. It means I have to think the unthinkable, speak the unspeakable, break the silence, acknowledge the elephant, and then take my share of responsibility for what comes next. It means I have to *do* something to create the possibility for my African American friend and me to have a conversation about race, gender, and us, rather than leave it to her to take all the risks and do all the work. The fact that it's so easy for me and other people in dominant groups not to do this is the single most powerful barrier to change. Understanding how to bring dominant groups into the conversation and the solution is the biggest challenge we face.

My work in this book is to help find a way to meet that challenge. It is to identify tools for understanding what's going on and what it's got to do with us without being swallowed up in a sea of guilt and blame or rushing into denial and angry self-defense. It is to open windows to new ways of thinking about difference and what's been made of it in this society. It is to remove barriers that stand between us and serious, long-term conversation *across* difference and effective action for change that can *make* a difference.

WE CAN'T TALK ABOUT IT
IF WE CAN'T USE THE WORDS

As I suggested in the opening pages of Chapter 1, you can't deal with a problem if you don't name it; once you name it, you can think, talk, and write about it. You can make sense of it by seeing how it's connected to other things that explain it and point toward solutions. Usually the language needed for this comes from people working to solve the problem, especially people most damaged by it. Words like *privilege, racism, sexism, anti-Semitism, heterosexism, classism, dominance, subordination, oppression,* and *patriarchy* are part of their everyday vocabulary.

When you name something, the word draws your attention to it, which makes you more likely to notice it as something significant. That's why most people have an immediate negative reaction to words like *racism, sexism,* or *privilege.* They don't want to look at what the words point to. Whites don't want to look at racism, nor men at sexism, nor heterosexuals at heterosexism, especially if they have worked hard to improve their class position. People don't want to look because they don't want to know what it has to do with them and how doing something about it might change not only the world, but themselves.

So people ignore the trouble by trying to get rid of the language that names it. They discredit the words or twist their meaning or turn them into a phobia or make them invisible. That's what's happened with most of the words that name the trouble around difference. It's become almost impossible, for example, to say *sexism* or *male privilege* without most men becoming so uncomfortable and defensive that conversation is impossible. They act as though *sexism* names a personality flaw found among men, and just saying the word ("Can we talk about sexism today?") is heard as an accusation of a personal moral failure. The same is true of all the other "isms." Since few people like to see themselves as bad, the words are taboo in "polite" company, including many diversity training programs at corporations and universities. So instead of talking about the racism and sexism that plague people's lives, people talk about "diversity" and "tolerance" and "appreciating difference." Those are good things to talk about, but they're not the same as the isms and the trouble they're connected to.

More than once, I've been asked to talk about the consequences of social domination, subordination, and oppression without actually saying the words *dominant, subordinate,* or *oppression.* At such times, I feel like a doctor trying to help a patient without ever mentioning the body or naming what's wrong. We can't get anywhere that way—and we haven't been. Our collective house is burning down, and we're tiptoeing around afraid to say "Fire."

The bottom line is that a trouble we can't talk about is a trouble we can't do anything about. Words like *sexism* and *privilege* point to something difficult and painful in our history that continues in everyday life in our society. That means there is no way to talk about it without difficulty and without pain. It is possible, however, to talk about it in ways that make the struggle and the pain worth it. To do that, however, we have to reclaim these lost and discredited words so that we can use them to name and make sense of the truth of what's going on.

Reclaiming the words begins with seeing that they rarely mean what most people think they mean. *Racist* isn't another word for "bad white people," just as *patriarchy* isn't a bit of nasty code for "men." *Oppression* and *dominance* name social realities that we can participate in without being oppressive or dominating *people*. And *feminism* isn't an ideology organized around being lesbian or hating men. But you'd never know it by listening to how these words are used in the mass media, popular culture, and over the dinner table. You'd never know such words could be part of a calm and responsible discussion of how to resolve a problem that belongs to all of us.

I use these difficult words freely in this book because I'm writing about the problems they name. Readers who happen to be white or male or heterosexual or economically comfortable or members of some other privileged category will have an easier time of it if they try to tolerate the discomfort such words evoke. I don't use them as accusations. (If I did, I'd have a hard time looking in the mirror each morning.) I don't intend that anyone take them personally. As a white, male, middle-class heterosexual, I know that in some ways these words are about me. There's no way to avoid playing some role in the troubles they name, and that's something I need to look at. But in equally important ways, the words are *not* about me because they name something much larger than me, something I didn't invent or create, but that was passed on to me as a legacy when I was born into this society. If I'm going to be part of the solution to that difficult legacy, it's important to step back from my defensive sensitivity to such language and look at the reality it points to. Then I can understand what it names and what it has to do with me and, most important, what I can do about it.

CHAPTER 3

The Trouble We're In
Privilege, Power, and Difference

The trouble around difference is really about privilege and power—the existence of privilege and the lopsided distribution of power that keeps it going. The trouble is rooted in a legacy we all inherited, and while we're here, it belongs to us. It isn't our fault. It wasn't caused by something we did or didn't do. But now that it's ours, it's up to us to decide how we're going to deal with it before we collectively pass it along to the generations that will follow ours.

Talking about power and privilege isn't easy, which is why people rarely do. The reason for this omission seems to be a great fear of anything that might make whites or males or heterosexuals uncomfortable or "pit groups against each other,"[1] even though groups are *already* pitted against one another by the structures of privilege that organize society as a whole. The fear keeps people from looking at what's going on and makes it impossible to do anything about the reality that lies deeper down, so that they can move toward the kind of world that would be better for everyone.

DIFFERENCE IS NOT THE PROBLEM

Ignoring privilege keeps us in a state of unreality, by promoting the illusion that difference by itself is the problem. In some ways, of course, it can be a problem when people try to work together across cultural divides that set groups up to think and do things their own way. But human beings have been overcoming such divides for thousands of years as a matter of routine. The real illusion connected to difference is the popular assumption that people are naturally afraid of what they don't know or understand. This supposedly makes it inevitable that you'll fear and distrust people who aren't like you and, in spite of your good intentions, you'll find it all but impossible to get along with them.

For all its popularity, the idea that everyone is naturally frightened by difference is a cultural myth that, more than anything, justifies keeping outsiders on the outside and treating them badly if they happen to get in. The mere fact that something is new or strange isn't enough to make us afraid of it. When Europeans first came to North America, for example, they weren't terribly afraid of the people they encountered, and the typical Native American response was to welcome these astonishingly "different" people with open arms (much to their later regret). Scientists, psychotherapists, inventors, novelists (and their fans), explorers, philosophers, spiritualists, anthropologists, and the just plain curious are all drawn toward the mystery of what they don't know. Even children—probably the most vulnerable form that people come in—seem to *love* the unknown, which is why parents are always worrying about what their toddler has gotten into *now*.

There is nothing inherently frightening about what we don't know. If we feel afraid, it isn't what we *don't* know that frightens us, it's what we think we *do* know. The problem is our ideas about what we don't know—what might happen next or what's lurking behind that unopened door or in the mind of the "strange"-looking guy sitting across from us on the nearly empty train. And how we think about such things isn't something we're born with. We learn to do it like we learn to tie our shoes, talk, and just about everything else. If we take difference and diversity as reasons for fear and occasions for trouble, it's because we've learned to think about them in ways that *make* for fear and trouble.

MAPPING DIFFERENCE: WHO ARE WE?

Issues of difference cover a large territory. A useful way to put it in perspective is with the "diversity wheel" (Figure 3.1) developed by Marilyn Loden and Judy Rosener.[2] In the hub of the wheel are six social characteristics: age, race, ethnicity, gender, physical ability and qualities (left/right-handedness, height, and so on), and sexual orientation. Around the outer ring are several others, including religion, marital status, whether we're parents, and social-class indicators such as education, occupation, and income.

Anyone can describe themselves by going around the wheel. Starting in the hub, I'm male, English-Norwegian (as far as I know), white (also as far as I know), fifty-four years old, heterosexual, and physically able (so far). In the outer ring, I'm married, a father, and a middle-class professional with a Ph.D. I've lived in New England for most of my life, but I've also lived in other countries. I have a vaguely Christian background, but if I had to identify my spiritual life with a particular tradition, I'd lean more toward Zen Buddhism than anything else. I served a brief stint in the Army reserves.

It would be useful if you stopped reading for a moment and do what I just did. Go around the diversity wheel and get a sense of yourself in terms of it.

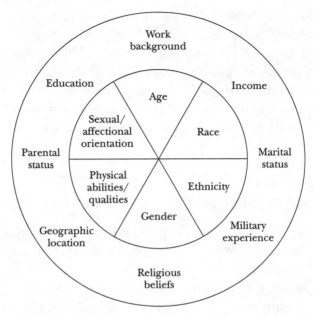

FIGURE 3.1 The Diversity Wheel. From *Workforce America* by M. Loden and J. Rosener, McGraw-Hill, 1991. Reproduced with permission from the McGraw-Hill Companies.

As you reflect on the results of this exercise, it might occur to you (as it did to me) that the wheel doesn't say much about the unique individual you know yourself to be, your personal history, the content of your character, what you dream and feel. It does, however, say a lot about the social reality that shapes everyone's life in powerful ways.

Imagine, for example, that you woke up tomorrow morning and found that your race was different from what it was when you went to bed (the plot of a 1970 movie called *Watermelon Man*). Or imagine that your gender or sexual orientation had changed (as happened to the central character in Virginia Woolf's novel *Orlando*). How would that affect how people perceive you and treat you? How would it affect how you see yourself? How would it change the material circumstances of your life, such as where you live or how much money you have? In what ways would the change make life better? Worse?

In answering these questions, try to go beyond the obvious consequences to see the ones that are perhaps more subtle. If you're heterosexual now, for example, and wake up gay or lesbian, your sexual feelings about women and men would be different. But what about how people perceive you and treat you in ways unrelated to sex? Would people treat you differently at school or work? Would friends treat you differently? Parents and siblings? Would you feel less included among friends? In similar ways, what changes would you experience in switching from female to male or from male to female, from white to African American, from Asian or Latina/o to Anglo, or from physically able to using a wheelchair? Again, focus on the social consequences, on how people would perceive you and treat you if such a thing happened to you. What opportunities would open or close? What rewards would or wouldn't come your way?

For most people, shifting only a few parts of the diversity wheel would be enough to change their lives dramatically. Even though the characteristics in the wheel may not tell us who we as individuals are in the privacy of our hearts and souls, they matter a great deal in our society because they locate us in relation to other people and the world in ways that have huge consequences.

The trouble around diversity, then, isn't just that people differ from one another. The trouble is produced by a world organized in ways that encourage people to *use* difference to include or exclude, reward or punish, credit or discredit, elevate or oppress, value or devalue, leave alone or harass.

This is especially true of the characteristics in the center of the wheel, which have the added quality of being almost impossible to change. It's true that sex-change surgery is available and that it's possible for some people to "pass" for a race or sexual orientation that is other than what they know themselves to be.

But this is quite different from being married one day and divorced the next, or getting a new job that suddenly elevates your class position. Unlike the outer portion of the wheel, the inner portion consists of characteristics that, one way or another, we must learn to live with regardless of how we choose to reveal ourselves to others.

People's perceptions are difficult to control, however, for they tend to assume that they can identify characteristics such as race and gender simply by looking at someone. We routinely form quick impressions of race, gender, age, or sexual orientation. Sometimes these impressions are based on blanket assumptions—that everyone, for example, is heterosexual until proven otherwise. Or if they *look* "white," they *are* white. People usually form such impressions without thinking, and they rely on them in order to see the world as an organized and predictable place from one moment to the next.

We may not realize how routinely we form such impressions until we run into someone who doesn't fit neatly into one of our categories, especially gender or sexual orientation. Pass someone on the street whom you can't identify as clearly male or female, for example, and it can jolt your attention and nag you until you think you've figured it out. Our culture allows for only two genders (compared with some cultures that recognize several), and anyone who doesn't clearly fit one or the other is instantly perceived as an outsider. This is why babies born with a mixture of sex characteristics are routinely altered surgically in order to "fit" the culturally defined categories of female and male. Most of our ways of thinking about sexuality are also based on social construction. Whether homosexual behavior is regarded as normal or deviant, for example, depends on the cultural context, as does the larger question of whether sexual orientation is perceived as defining the kind of human being you are and the way you live your life.

So the characteristics at the center of the wheel are very hard to change, are the object of quick and firm impressions, and can profoundly affect our lives. Clearly, diversity isn't just about the "variety" that the word suggests. Diversity *could* just be about that, but only in some other world.[3]

THE SOCIAL CONSTRUCTION
OF DIFFERENCE

The African American novelist James Baldwin once wrote an essay in which he offered the provocative idea that there is no such thing as whiteness or, for that matter, blackness or, more generally, race. "No one is white before he/she came to America," he wrote. "It took generations, and a vast amount of coercion, before this became a white country."[4]

What did Baldwin mean? In the simplest sense, he was pointing to a basic aspect of social reality: Most of what we experience as "real" is a cultural creation. In other words, it's made up, even though we don't experience it that way.

Take race, for example. Baldwin isn't denying the reality that skin pigmentation varies from one person to another. What he is saying is that unless you live in a culture that recognizes those differences as significant and meaningful, they are socially irrelevant and therefore do not exist. A "black woman" in Africa, therefore, who has not experienced white racism, does not *think* of herself as black or experience herself as black, nor do the people around her. African, yes; a woman, yes. But not as a *black* woman.

When she comes to the United States, however, where privilege is organized according to race, suddenly she becomes black because people assign her to a social category that bears that name, and they treat her differently as a result. In similar ways, a Norwegian farmer has no reason to think of himself as white so long as he's in Norway. But when he comes to the United States, one of the first things he discovers is the significance of being considered white and the privileges that go along with it. And so he is eager to adopt "white" as part of his identity and to make sure that others acknowledge it.

So Baldwin is telling us that race and all its categories have no significance outside of systems of privilege and oppression, and it is these systems that created them.[5] This is what sociologists call the "social construction" of reality.

One way to see the constructed nature of reality is to notice how the definitions of different "races" change historically, by including groups at one time that were excluded in another. The Irish, for example, were long considered by the dominant white Anglo-Saxon Protestants of England and the United States to be members of a nonwhite "race," as were Italians, Jews, and people from a number of Eastern European countries. As such, immigrants from these groups to England and the United States were excluded and subjugated and exploited in much the same way that blacks were. This was especially true of the Irish in Ireland in relation to the British, who for centuries treated them as an inferior race. Note, however, that their skin color was indistinguishable from that of those considered to be "white." If anything, the skin of most people of Irish descent is "fairer" than that of others of European heritage. But their actual complexion didn't matter, because the dominant racial group has the cultural authority to define the boundaries around "white" as it chooses.

What makes socially constructed reality so powerful is that we rarely if ever experience it as that. We think the way our culture defines race or gender or sexual orientation is simply the way things are in some objective sense. We think there really is such a thing as "race" and that the words we use simply name an objective reality that is "out there." The truth is, however, that once human beings give something a name—whether it be skin color or whom you like to sleep with—that thing acquires a significance it otherwise would not have. More important, the name quickly takes on a life of its own as we forget the social process that created it and start treating it as "real" in and of itself.

This process is what allows us to believe that something like "race" actually points to a set of clear and unambiguous categories into which people fall, ignoring the fact that the definition of various races changes all the time and is riddled with inconsistencies and overlapping boundaries. But when the stakes are privilege and power, dominant groups are quite willing to ignore such inconsistencies so long as the result is a continuation of their privilege.

WHAT IS PRIVILEGE?

No matter what privileged group you belong to, if you want to understand the problem of privilege and difference, the first stumbling block is usually the idea of privilege itself. When people hear that they belong to a privileged group or benefit from something like "race privilege" or "gender privilege," they don't get it, or they feel angry and defensive about what they do get. *Privilege* has become one of those loaded words we need to reclaim so that we can use it to name and illuminate the truth. Denying that privilege exists is a serious barrier to change, so serious that it is the subject of a whole chapter (Chapter 8). But for now, it's important to get a sense of what the word means before we go any further.

As Peggy McIntosh describes it, privilege exists when one group has something of value that is denied to others simply because of the groups they belong to, rather than because of anything they've done or failed to do.[6] If people take me more seriously when I give a speech than they would someone of color saying the same things in the same way, for example, then

I'm benefiting from white privilege. That a heterosexual black woman can feel free to talk about her life in ways that reveal the fact that she's married to a man is a form of heterosexual privilege because lesbians and gay men cannot casually reveal their sexual orientation without putting themselves at risk.

Notice that in all these examples, it's relatively easy for people to be unaware of how privilege affects them. When people come up to me after I give a speech, for example, it doesn't occur to me that they'd probably be more critical and less positive if I were Latino or a woman or gay. I don't *feel* privileged in that moment. I just feel that I did a good job, and I enjoy the rewards that are supposed to go with it.

The existence of privilege doesn't mean I *didn't* do a good job, of course, or that I don't deserve credit for it. What it does mean is that I'm *also* getting something that other people are denied, people who are like me in every respect except for the gender, race, and sexual orientation categories they belong to. In this sense, my privileged status doesn't determine my outcomes, but it is definitely an *asset* that makes it more likely that whatever talent, ability, and aspirations I have will result in something good for me.[7] In the same way, being female, or of color, or homosexual doesn't determine people's outcomes, but they are turned into *liabilities* that make it less likely that their talent, ability, and aspirations will be recognized and rewarded.

 The ease of not being aware of privilege is an aspect of privilege itself, what some call "the luxury of obliviousness" (or what philosophers call "epistemic privilege"). Awareness requires effort and commitment. Being able to command the attention of lower-status individuals without having to give it in return is a key aspect of privilege. African Americans, for example, have to pay close attention to whites and white culture and get to know them well enough to avoid displeasing them, since whites control jobs, schools, the police, and most other resources and sources of power. Race privilege gives whites little reason to pay a lot of attention to African Americans or to how white privilege affects them. In other words, "To be white in America means not having to think about it."[8] We could say the same thing about maleness or heterosexuality or any other basis for privilege. So strong is the sense of entitlement behind this luxury that males, whites, and others can feel put upon in the face of even the mildest invitation to pay attention to issues of privilege. "We shouldn't *have* to look at this stuff," they seem to say. "It isn't *fair.*"

Two Types of Privilege

According to McIntosh, privilege comes in two types. The first is based on what she calls "unearned entitlements," which are things that all people *should* have, such as feeling safe in public spaces or working in a place where they feel they belong and are valued for what they can contribute. When an unearned entitlement is restricted to certain groups, however, it becomes a form of privilege she calls "unearned advantage."

In some cases, it's possible to do away with unearned advantages without anyone's having to lose out. If the workplace changed so that *everyone* was valued for what they could contribute, for example, that privilege would disappear without the dominant groups' having to give up their own sense that *they* are valued for their contributions. The unearned entitlement would then be available to all and, as such, would no longer be a form of unearned advantage.

In many other cases, however, unearned advantages give dominant groups a competitive edge they are reluctant to even acknowledge, much less give up. This is particularly true of lower-, working-, and lower-middle-class whites and males who know all too well the price they pay for a lack of class privilege and how hard it is to improve their lives and hang on to what they've managed to achieve. Their lack of class privilege, however, can blind them to the fact that the cultural valuing of whiteness and maleness over color and femaleness gives them an edge in most situations that involve evaluations of credibility or competence. To give up that advantage would double or even triple the amount of competition. This would especially affect white males, who are a shrinking numerical minority of the U.S. population. A loss of race and gender privilege would level the playing field to admit white women and people of color, a combined group that outnumbers white males by a large margin.

The other form of privilege—what McIntosh calls "conferred dominance"—goes a step further by giving one group power over another. The common pattern of men controlling conversations with women, for example, is grounded in a cultural assumption that men are supposed to dominate women. An adolescent boy who appears too willing to defer to his mother risks being called a "mama's boy," in the same way that a husband who appears in any way subordinate to his wife is often labeled "henpecked" (or worse). The counterpart for girls carries no such stigma. "Daddy's girl" isn't considered an insult in this culture, and the language contains *no* specific insulting terms for a wife who is under the control of her husband.

Conferred dominance also manifests itself in race privilege. In his book *The Rage of a Privileged Class,* for example, the African American journalist Ellis Cose tells the story of an African American lawyer, a partner in a large firm, who goes to the office early one Saturday morning to catch up on some work and is confronted near the elevator by a recently hired young white attorney.

"Can I help you?" the white man says pointedly.

The partner shakes his head and tries to pass, but the white man steps in his way and repeats what is now a challenge to the man's very presence in the building: "Can I *help* you?" Only then does the partner reveal his identity to the young man, who then steps aside to let him pass. The young white man had no reason to assume the right to control the older man standing before him, except the reason provided by the cultural assumption of white racial dominance that can override any class advantage a person of color might have.[9]

The milder forms of unearned advantage usually change first because they are the easiest for privileged groups to give up. Over the last several decades, for example, national surveys show a steady decline in the percentage of whites in the United States who express overtly racist attitudes toward people of color. This trend is reflected in diversity training programs that usually focus on appreciating or at least tolerating differences—in other words, extending unearned entitlements to everyone instead of the dominant group alone.

It's much harder, however, to do something about power and the unequal distribution of resources and rewards. This is why issues of conferred dominance and the stronger forms of unearned advantage get much less attention, and why, when they are raised, they often provoke hostile defensiveness, especially from those who struggle with a lack of class privilege. Perhaps more than any other factor, this reluctance to come to terms with more serious and entrenched forms of privilege is why most diversity programs produce limited and short-lived results.

What Privilege Looks Like in Everyday Life

In one way or another, privilege shows up in the daily details of people's lives in almost every social setting. Consider the following examples of race privilege.[10] This is a long list because the details of people's lives are many and varied. Resist the temptation to go through it quickly. Take your time and try to identify situations in which each might occur.

- Whites are less likely than blacks to be arrested; once arrested, they are less likely to be convicted and, once convicted, less likely to go to prison, regardless of the crime or circumstances. Whites, for example, constitute 90 percent of those who use illegal drugs, but less than half of those in prison on drug-use charges are white.

- Although many superstar professional athletes are black, in general black players are held to higher standards than whites. It is easier for a "good, but not great" white player to make a professional team than it is for a similar black.

- Whites are more likely than comparable blacks to have loan applications approved, and less likely to be given poor information or the runaround during the application process.

- Whites are charged lower prices for new and used cars than people of color are, and because of residential segregation whites have access to higher-quality goods of all kinds at cheaper prices.

- Whites can choose whether to be conscious of their racial identity or to ignore it and regard themselves as simply human beings.

- Whites are more likely to control conversations and be allowed to get away with it, and to have their ideas and contributions taken seriously, including those that were suggested previously by a person of color and dismissed.

- Whites can usually assume that national heroes, success models, and other figures held up for general admiration will be of their race.

- Whites can generally assume that when they go out in public, they won't be challenged and asked to explain what they're doing, nor will they be attacked by hate groups simply because of their race.

- Whites can assume that when they go shopping, they'll be treated as serious customers, not as potential shoplifters or people without the money to make a purchase. When they try to cash a check or use a credit card, they can assume they won't be hassled for additional identification and will be given the benefit of the doubt.

- White representation in government and the ruling circles of corporations, universities, and other organizations is disproportionately high.

- Most whites are not segregated into communities that isolate them from the best job opportunities, schools, and community services.

- Whites have greater access to quality education and health care.

- Whites are more likely to be given early opportunities to show what they can do at work, to be identified as potential candidates for promotion, to be mentored, to be given a second chance when they fail, and to be allowed to treat failure as a learning experience rather than as an indication of who they are and the shortcomings of their race.

- Whites can assume that race won't be used to predict whether they'll fit in at work or whether teammates will feel comfortable working with them.

- Whites can succeed without other people's being surprised.

- Whites don't have to deal with an endless and exhausting stream of attention to their race. They can simply take their race for granted as unremarkable to the extent of experiencing themselves as not even having a race. Unlike some of my African American students, for example, I don't have people coming up to me and treating me as if I were some exotic "other," gushing about how "cool" or different I am, wanting to know where I'm "from," and reaching out to touch my hair.

- Whites don't find themselves slotted into occupations identified with their race like blacks are slotted into support positions or Asians into engineering, for example.

- Whites aren't confused with other whites, as if all whites look alike. They're noticed for their individuality, and they take offense whenever they're characterized as members of a category (such as "white") rather than being perceived and treated as individuals.

- Whites can reasonably expect that if they work hard and "play by the rules," they'll get what they deserve, and they feel justified in complaining if they don't. It is something other racial groups cannot realistically expect.

In the following list for gender privilege, note how some items repeat from the list on race, but that other items do not.

- In most professions and upper-level occupations, men are held to a lower standard than women. It is easier for a "good but not great" male lawyer to make partner than it is for a comparable woman.

- Men are charged lower prices for new and used cars.

- If men do poorly at something or make a mistake or commit a crime, they can generally assume that people won't attribute the failure to their gender. The kids who shoot teachers and schoolmates are almost always boys, but rarely is the fact that all of this violence is being done by males raised as an important issue.

- Men can usually assume that national heroes, success models, and other figures held up for general admiration will be men.

- Men can generally assume that when they go out in public, they won't be sexually harassed or assaulted, and if they are victimized, they won't be asked to explain what they were doing there.

- Male representation in government and the ruling circles of corporations and other organizations is disproportionately high.

- Men are more likely to be given early opportunities to show what they can do at work, to be identified as potential candidates for promotion, to be mentored, to be given a second chance when they fail, and to be allowed to treat failure as a learning experience rather than as an indication of who they are and the shortcomings of their gender.

- Men are more likely than women to control conversations and be allowed to get away with it, and to have their ideas and contributions taken seriously, even those that were suggested previously by a woman and dismissed or ignored.

- Most men can assume that their gender won't be used to determine whether they'll fit in at work or whether teammates will feel comfortable working with them.

- Men can succeed without others' being surprised.

- Men don't have to deal with an endless and exhausting stream of attention drawn to their gender (for example, to how sexually attractive they are).

- Men don't find themselves slotted into a narrow range of occupations identified with their gender like women are slotted into community relations, human resources, social work, elementary school teaching, librarianship, nursing, clerical and secretarial.

- Men can reasonably expect that if they work hard and "play by the rules," they'll get what they deserve, and they feel justified in complaining if they don't.

- The standards used to evaluate men as *men* are consistent with the standards used to evaluate them in other roles such as occupations. Standards used to evaluate women as women are often different from those used to evaluate them in other roles. For example, a man can be both a "real man" and a successful and aggressive lawyer, while an aggressive woman lawyer may succeed as a lawyer but be judged as not measuring up as a woman.

In the following list regarding sexual orientation, note again items in common with the other two lists and items peculiar to this form of privilege.

- Heterosexuals are free to reveal and live their intimate relationships openly—by referring to their partners by name, recounting experiences, going out in public together, displaying pictures on their desks at work—without being accused of "flaunting" their sexuality or risking discrimination.

- Heterosexuals can rest assured that whether they're hired, promoted, or fired from a job will have nothing to do with their sexual orientation, an aspect of themselves they cannot change.

- Heterosexuals can move about in public without fear of being harassed or physically attacked because of their sexual orientation.

- Heterosexuals don't run the risk of being reduced to a single aspect of their lives, as if being heterosexual summed up the kind of person they are. Instead, they can be viewed and treated as complex human beings who happen to be heterosexual.

- Heterosexuals can usually assume that national heroes, success models, and other figures held up for general admiration will be assumed to be heterosexual.

- Most heterosexuals can assume that their sexual orientation won't be used to determine whether they'll fit in at work or whether teammates will feel comfortable working with them.

- Heterosexuals don't have to worry that their sexual orientation will be used as a weapon against them, to undermine their achievements or power.

- Heterosexuals can turn on the television or go to the movies and be assured of seeing characters, news reports, and stories that reflect the reality of their lives.

- Heterosexuals can live where they want without having to worry about neighbors who disapprove of their sexual orientation.

- Heterosexuals can live in the comfort of knowing that other people's assumptions about their sexual orientation are correct.

Regardless of which group we're talking about, privilege generally allows people to assume a certain level of acceptance, inclusion, and respect in the world, to operate within a relatively wide comfort zone. Privilege increases the odds of having things your own way, of being able to set the agenda in a social situation and determine the rules and standards and how they're applied. Privilege grants the cultural authority to make judgments about others and to have those judgments stick. It allows people to define reality and to have prevailing definitions of reality fit their experience. Privilege means being able to decide who gets taken seriously, who receives attention, who is accountable to whom and for what. And it grants a presumption of superiority and social permission to act on that presumption without having to worry about being challenged.

To have privilege is to be allowed to move through your life without being marked in ways that identify you as an outsider, as exceptional or "other" to be excluded, or to be included but always with conditions. As Paul Kivel points out, "In the United States, a person is considered a member of the lowest status group from which they have any heritage."[11] This means that if you come from several ethnic groups, the one that lowers your status is the one you're most likely to be tagged with, as in "She's part Jewish," or "He's part Vietnamese," but rarely "She's part white." In fact, having any black ancestry is still enough to be classified as *entirely* black in many people's eyes (in accordance with the "one drop rule" that has been a striking feature of race relations in the United States for several centuries). People are tagged with other labels that point to the lowest-status group they belong to, as in "woman doctor" or "black writer," but never "white lawyer" or "male senator." Any category that lowers our status relative to others' can be used to mark us; to be privileged is to go through life with the relative ease of being unmarked.[12]

If you're male or heterosexual or white and you find yourself shaking your head at the foregoing descriptions of privilege— "This isn't true for *me*"—it might be due to the complex and sometimes paradoxical way that privilege works in social life.

PRIVILEGE AS PARADOX

Individuals are the ones who experience privilege or the lack of it, but individuals aren't what is actually privileged. Instead, privilege is defined in relation to a group or social category. In other words, race privilege is more about *white* people than it is about white *people*. I'm not race privileged because of who I am as a person. Whiteness is privileged in this society, and I have access to that privilege only when people identify me as belonging to the category "white." I do or don't receive race privilege based on which category people put me in without their knowing a single other thing about me.

This means that you don't actually have to be white or male or heterosexual to receive the privilege attached to those categories. All you have to do is convince people you belong to the appropriate category. The film *Shakespeare in Love,* for example, is set in Elizabethan England, where acting on the stage was a privilege reserved for men. The character Viola (the woman Shakespeare falls in love with) wants more than anything to act on the stage, and finally realizes her dream not by changing her sex and becoming a man, but by successfully presenting herself as one. That's all that it takes.

In similar ways, you can lose privilege if people think you don't belong to a particular category. My sexual orientation is heterosexual, for example, which entitles me to heterosexual privilege, but only if people identify me as heterosexual. If I were to announce to everyone that I'm gay, I would immediately lose my access to heterosexual privilege (unless people refused to believe me), even though I would still be, in fact, a heterosexual person. As Charlotte Bunch put it, "If you don't have a sense of what privilege is, I suggest that you go home and announce to everybody that you know—a roommate, your family, the people you work with—that you're a queer. Trying being queer for a week."[13] When it comes to privilege, then, it doesn't really matter who we really are. What matters is who other people *think* we are, which is to say, the social categories they put us in.

Several important consequences follow from this paradox of privilege. First, privilege is rooted in societies and organizations as much as it's rooted in people's personalities and how they perceive and react to one another. This means that doing something about the problem of privilege takes more than changing individuals. As Harry Brod wrote about gender privilege:

> We need to be clear that there is no such thing as giving up one's privilege to be "outside" the system. One is always *in* the system. The only question is whether one is part of the system in a way which challenges or strengthens the status quo. Privilege is not something I *take* and which I therefore have the option of *not* taking. It is something that society *gives* me, and unless I change the institutions which give it to me, they will continue to give it, and I will continue to *have* it, however noble and egalitarian my intentions.[14]

Societies and organizations promote privilege in complicated ways, which we'll look at in later chapters. For now, it's important to be aware that we don't have to be special or even feel special in order to have access to privilege, because privilege doesn't derive from who we are or what we've done. It is a social arrangement that depends on which category we happen to be sorted into by other people and how they treat us as a result.

The paradoxical experience of *being* privileged without *feeling* privileged is a second consequence of the fact that privilege is more about social categories than who people are. It has to do primarily with the people we use as standards of comparison— what sociologists call "reference groups." We use reference groups to construct a sense of how good or bad, high or low we are in the scheme of things. To do this, we usually don't look downward in the social hierarchy but to people we identify as being on the same level as or higher level than our own. So pointing out to someone in the United States who lives in poverty that they're better off than impoverished people in India doesn't make them feel much better, because people in the United States don't use Indians as a reference group.

Instead, they will compare themselves with those who seem like them in key respects and see if they're doing better or worse than *them.*

Since being white is valued in this society, whites will tend to compare themselves with other whites, not with people of color. In the same way, men will tend to compare themselves with other men and not with women. What this means, however, is that whites will tend not to feel privileged *by their race* when they compare themselves with their reference group, because their reference group is also white. In the same way, men won't feel privileged *by their gender* in comparison with other men, because gender doesn't elevate them above other *men.* A partial exception to this is the hierarchy that exists among men between heterosexuals and homosexuals: heterosexual men are more likely to consider themselves "real men" and therefore socially valued above gay men. But even here, the mere fact of being male isn't experienced as a form of privilege, because gay men are also male.

An exception to these patterns can occur for those who are privileged by gender or race but find themselves ranked low in terms of social class. To protect themselves from feeling and being seen as on the bottom of the ladder, they may go out of their way to compare themselves to women or people of color by emphasizing their supposed gender or racial superiority. This can appear as an exaggerated sense of masculinity, for example, or as overt attempts to put women or people of color "in their place," including by harassment, violence, or behavior that is openly contemptuous or demeaning.

A corollary to being privileged without knowing it is to be on the *other* side of privilege without necessarily feeling *that.* For example, I sometimes hear a woman say something like, "I've never been oppressed as a woman." Often this is said to challenge the idea that male privilege exists at all. But this confuses the social position of females and males as social categories with one woman's subjective experience of belonging to one of those categories. They aren't the same. For various reasons—including social-class privilege or an unusual family experience or simply being young—she may have avoided a direct confrontation with many of the consequences of being female in a society that privileges maleness. Or she may have managed to overcome them to a degree that she doesn't feel hampered by them. Or she may be engaging in denial. Or she may be unaware of how she is discriminated against (unaware, perhaps, that being a woman is the reason her professors ignore her in class) or may have so internalized her subordinate status that she doesn't see it as a problem (thinking, perhaps, that women are ignored because they aren't intelligent enough to say anything worth listening to). Regardless of what her experience is based on, it is just that—her experience—and it doesn't have to square with the larger social reality that everyone (including her) must deal with one way or another. It's like living in a rainy climate and somehow avoiding being rained on yourself. It's still a rainy place to be and getting wet is something most people have to deal with.

The Paradox That Privilege Doesn't Necessarily Make You Happy

I often hear men deny the existence of male privilege by saying they don't feel happy or fulfilled in their own lives. They reason that you can't be both privileged and miserable, or, as one man put it, "Privilege means 'having all the goodies,'" so if you don't feel good, then you must not be privileged.

This is a common reaction that is related to the difference between individuals on the one hand and social categories on the other. Knowing that someone belongs to one or more of the privileged categories, "white," or "heterosexual," or "male," doesn't tell us what life is actually like for them. Belonging to a privileged category improves the odds in favor of certain kinds of advantages and preferential treatment, but it doesn't guarantee anything for any given individual. Being born white, male, and upper-class, for example, is a powerful combination of privileged categories that would certainly put a person in line for all kinds of valued things. But they could still wind up losing it all in the stock market and living under a bridge in a cardboard box. Nonetheless, even though the privilege attached to race, gender, and social class didn't work out for *them,* the privilege itself still exists as a fact of social life.

Another reason privilege and happiness often don't go together is that privilege can exact a cost from those who have it. To have privilege is to participate in a system that confers advantage and dominance at the expense of other people, and that can cause distress to those who benefit from it. White privilege, for example, comes at a huge cost to people of color, and on some level white people must struggle with this knowledge. That's where all the guilt comes from and the lengths to which white people will go to avoid feeling and looking at it. In similar ways, male privilege exacts a cost as men compete with other men and strive to prove their manhood so that they can continue to be counted among "real men" who are worthy of being set apart from—and above—women. It should come as no surprise that men often feel unhappy and that they associate their unhappiness with the fact of being men.

OPPRESSION: THE FLIP SIDE
OF PRIVILEGE

For every social category that is privileged, one or more other categories are oppressed in relation to it. The concept of oppression points to social forces that tend to "press" upon people and hold them down, to hem them in and block their pursuit of a good life. Just as privilege tends to open doors of opportunity, oppression tends to slam them shut.[15]

Like privilege, oppression results from the social relationship between privileged and oppressed categories, which makes it possible for individuals to vary in their personal experience of being oppressed ("I've never been oppressed as a woman"). This also means, however, that in order to have the experience of being oppressed, it is necessary to belong to an oppressed category. In other words, men cannot be oppressed *as men,* just as whites cannot be oppressed as whites or heterosexuals as heterosexuals because a group can be oppressed only if there exists another group that has the power to oppress them.

As we saw earlier, people in privileged categories can certainly feel bad in ways that can resemble oppression. Men, for example, can feel burdened by what they take to be their responsibility to provide for their families. Or they can feel limited and even damaged by the requirement that "real men" must avoid expressing feelings other than anger. But although belonging to a privileged category costs them something that may *feel* oppressive, to call it oppression distorts the nature of what is happening to them and why.

It ignores, for example, the fact that the cost of male privilege is far outweighed by the benefits, while the oppressive cost of being female is not outweighed by corresponding benefits. Misapplying the label of "oppression" also tempts us into the false argument that if men and women are *both* oppressed because of gender, then one oppression balances out the other and no privilege can be said to exist. So when we try to label the pain that men feel because of gender (or that whites feel because of racism, and so on), whether we call it "oppression" or simply "pain" makes a huge difference in how we perceive the world and how it works.

The complexity of systems of privilege makes it possible, of course, for men to experience oppression if they also happen to be people of color or gay or in a lower social class, but not because they are male. In the same way, whites can experience oppression as women, homosexuals, or members of lower social classes, but not because they're white.

Note also that because oppression results from relations between social categories, it is not possible to be oppressed by society itself. Living in a particular society can make people feel miserable, but we can't call that misery "oppression" unless it arises from being on the losing end in a system of privilege. That can't happen in relation to society as a whole, because a society isn't something that can be the recipient of privilege. Only people can do this by belonging to privileged categories in relation to other categories that aren't.

Finally, it's important to point out that belonging to a privileged category that has an oppressive relationship with another isn't the same as being an oppressive *person* who behaves in oppressive ways. That whites as a social category oppress people of color as a social category, for example, is a social fact. That doesn't, however, tell us how a particular white *person* thinks or feels about particular people of color or behaves toward them. This can be a subtle distinction to hang on to, but hang on to it we must if we're going to maintain a clear idea of what oppression is and how it works.

CHAPTER 4

Capitalism, Class, and the Matrix of Domination

Every year I team-teach a course on race, and there always comes a point in the semester when students start saying things like this: "We don't get it. If race is socially constructed and doesn't exist otherwise, and if human beings aren't bound to be terrified of one another, then where does racism come from? Why all the oppression and hostility and violence over something that's been made up? And why would people make it up this way in the first place? It's stupid."

The answer we give takes us into the history of race, where we find two things that usually startle them as much as they did me when I first became aware of them. First, white racism hasn't been around very long—hardly more than several centuries and certainly not as long as white people have been aware of other races. Second, its appearance in Europe and the Americas occurred right along with the expansion of capitalism as an economic system. This is no coincidence, because capitalism played a major role in the development of white privilege, and still plays a major role in its perpetuation.

This isn't surprising given the importance of economics in social life, which is, after all, how people organize themselves to provide what they need for their material existence—food, shelter, clothing, and the like—and to live what their culture defines as a "good life." Because economic systems are the source of wealth, they are also the basis for every social institution, since the state and church and universities and the like cannot survive without an economic base. It takes a great deal of material and labor to build a cathedral or a university, for example, or to pay for political campaigns or equip and feed a police force or an army. This means that the central place of economics in social life gives individuals and systems powerful reasons to go along with the dominant economic system. Capitalism has been that system for the last several hundreds years, and today, with the demise of the Soviet Union, it's virtually the only game in town.

What, then, did capitalism have to do with the origins of white racism? In the simplest sense, it was a matter of economics. Understanding why begins with understanding capitalism itself.[1]

HOW CAPITALISM WORKS

The basic goal of modern capitalism is to turn money into more money. Capitalists invest money to buy what it takes to produce goods and services: raw materials, machinery, electricity, buildings, and, of course, human labor. It doesn't matter what they produce so long as they can find a market in which to sell it at a profit—for more than it cost to have it produced—and end up with more money than they started with. Whether the result enhances human life (providing healthy food, affordable housing, health care, and the like) or causes harm (tobacco, alcohol, drugs, weapons, slavery, pollution) may be an issue for individual capitalists who value a clear conscience. But the system itself doesn't depend on such moral or ethical considerations, for profit is profit and there's no way to tell "good" money from "bad." Even the damage done by one enterprise can serve as a source of profit for another. Industrial pollution, for example, creates profitable opportunities for companies that specialize in cleaning it up.

Capitalists employ workers to produce goods and services, paying them wages in exchange for their time. Capitalists then sell the goods and services that workers produce. For capitalists to make a living (since they don't produce anything themselves), they have to get workers to produce goods and services that are worth more than the wages capitalists pay them. The difference is what capitalists live on.

Why, however, would workers accept wages worth less than the value of what they produce? The general answer is that they don't have much choice, because under capitalism the tools and factories used to produce goods aren't owned by the people who actually do the work. Instead, they're owned by capitalists, especially stockholders who invest in companies. So, for most people who want to earn a living, chances are they'll have to work for one capitalist employer or another, which means choosing between working on the capitalist's terms or not working at all. As corporate capitalism has extended its reach into every area of social life, even professionals now have to confront this choice. Physicians, for example, who were once regarded as the model of an independent profession, are increasingly compelled to become what are essentially highly paid employees of health maintenance organizations. As a result, they have recently begun to lobby Congress for the right to engage in collective bargaining with HMOs—in other words, to form a labor union for physicians.[2]

Since capitalists profit from the difference between the cost of producing goods (most of which is people's labor) and what they can sell goods for in markets, the cheaper the labor, the more money left over for them. This is why capitalists are so concerned about increasing "worker productivity"—finding ways for workers to produce more goods for the same or less pay. One way to accomplish this is through the use of technology, especially machines that replace people altogether. Another is to threaten to close down or relocate businesses if workers won't make concessions on wages, health and retirement benefits, job security, and working conditions. A third and increasingly popular strategy in the "new global economy" is to move production to countries where people are willing to work for less than they are in Europe or North America and where authoritarian governments will control workers and discourage the formation of unions and other sources of organized resistance, often with the direct support of the U.S. government.[3]

CAPITALISM AND CLASS

The dynamics of capitalism produce not only enormous amounts of wealth, but high—and increasing—levels of inequality, both within societies and globally. The richest 10 percent of the U.S. population holds more than two-thirds of all the wealth, including almost 90 percent of cash, almost half the land, more than 90 percent of business assets, and almost all stocks and bonds.[4] In 1998, the richest top 20 percent of all households received almost *half* of all income, and the richest 40 percent received almost *three-quarters,* leaving just a quarter of all income to be divided among the remaining 60 percent of all households.[5]

Such patterns of inequality result from and perpetuate a class system based on widening gaps in income, wealth, and power between those on top and everyone below them.[6] It is a system that produces oppressive consequences. For those at the bottom, the costs are enormous, with living conditions among the rural poor, for example, at or below the level found in many of the world's most impoverished nonindustrial societies.[7] Even among employed members of the working class, as well as many of those in the middle class, the class system offers little security and takes an emotional toll. A great many jobs are boring, mind-numbing, and make use of much less than what most people have to offer. And the vast majority of working people have little if any control over the work they do or whether they keep their jobs.

It also doesn't take much to see that with the bottom 60 percent of the U.S. population having to divide just a quarter of all income among themselves, there isn't going to be enough to go around. While capitalism produces an overall abundance of goods and services, it distributes that wealth so unequally that it also produces conditions of scarcity for most of the population. This makes life for those 150 million or so people an ongoing competition that is full of anxiety and struggle. For a majority of people, it wouldn't take very much—a divorce, perhaps, or a serious illness or being laid off—to substantially lower their standard of living, even to the extent of putting them out of their homes and onto welfare.[8]

The "American Dream" aside, most people also have relatively little power to improve their class position. Much of the increase in household wealth, for example, has been based on a growing mountain of credit card debt, people working two or more jobs, and families relying on two wage earners to support the same standard of living their parents managed with one. Although unemployment is at record low levels, most of the new jobs that have been created over the last several decades have been low-paying and with little chance of advancement. In addition, studies of occupational mobility show most people are as likely to move downward as they are upward in the class system.[9] Because of this and the widening gulf separating the upper class from everyone else, the middle class has actually shrunk.[10] Since 1964, the percentage of people who see themselves as middle class has fallen from 61 to 45, while the percentage seeing themselves as working class has risen from 35 to 44.[11]

In short, in an era of continuing corporate downsizing, the flight of well-paying industrial jobs overseas, and the rapid growth of low-level service occupations, for most people the struggle to move upward rarely gets much beyond hanging on to what they have.[12] There is, of course, upward movement by some, but outside of high-technology fields that are currently in demand, this almost always comes at the expense of others who must move down to make room for them. This creates what economist Lester Thurow calls a "zero-sum" society, adapting a term used to describe games that are designed so that one person's gain is always someone else's loss.[13] This makes it inevitable that at any given moment a substantial proportion of the population will have to live in poverty or close to it. But it also sets the stage for different groups within the "bottom" 60 percent to see one another as competitors and threats to their livelihood.

As we'll see below, such dynamics of capitalism have played a key role in the trouble around difference and privilege, especially in relation to race and gender.

CAPITALISM, DIFFERENCE, AND PRIVILEGE: RACE AND GENDER

Given how capitalism works, it connects to white racism in ways that are both direct and indirect. In the history of the United States, the direct connection is most apparent in the enslavement of millions of Africans as a source of cheap labor on cotton and tobacco plantations in the South. This was done for purely economic reasons, as became dramatically apparent after Eli Whitney's invention of the cotton gin in 1792 made it possible to process many times more cotton than before. Tempted by the potential to multiply cotton production—and profits—many times over, planters chose to minimize labor costs by exploiting slave labor rather than pay free workers a living wage.

As a result, the number of enslaved blacks in the United States jumped from 1 million in 1800 to almost 4 million in 1860, just before the start of the Civil War.[14] The primacy of profit in white thinking was also apparent in the reactions of businesses that relied on paid white workers. They didn't object to slavery on moral grounds. Instead, they complained that slave owners were engaging in unfair competition because their labor costs were so low it was impossible to compete against them. It was common, for example, for construction firms that depended on slave labor to win contracts away from their competition by underbidding them.[15]

Following the Civil War, the capitalist appetite for cheap agricultural labor was no less than before, and freed blacks were held in a new form of bondage by an oppressive system of tenant farming that kept them perpetually in debt.[16] Beyond the South, the profitability of racism showed itself in the widespread use of Chinese immigrant labor to build the Western railways under harsh and demeaning conditions. Even farther west, Japanese immigrants had similar experiences on the sugar and pineapple plantations of Hawaii.[17]

Capitalism's direct connection to white racism has also operated in the acquisition of land and raw materials which, like cheap labor, play a key role in the rapid growth of industry and wealth. In the heyday of capitalist expansion during the eighteenth and nineteenth centuries, Europe and then the United States found an abundance of what they needed in Africa, Asia, and the Americas. To acquire them, they relied on varying combinations of military conquest, political domination, and economic exploitation.[18] They were spectacularly successful at it, especially Great Britain, a small island nation with few natural resources of its own that nonetheless managed to become the world's first true industrial power. Unlike Britain, the United States was already rich in natural resources, but whites could get at them only by taking them away from the

Native American tribes who inhabited most of the land as well as from Mexico, which encompassed most of what is now the far western and southwestern United States. Whites managed to take what they wanted through a combination of conquest, genocide, and a complex array of treaties that were routinely ignored.[19]

To justify such direct forms of imperialism and oppression, whites developed the *idea* of whiteness to define a privileged social category elevated above everyone who wasn't included in it.[20] This made it possible to reconcile conquest, treachery, slavery, and genocide with the nation's newly professed ideals of democracy, freedom, and human dignity. If whiteness defined what it meant to be human, then it was seen as less of an offense against the Constitution (not to mention God) to dominate and oppress those who happened to fall outside that definition as the United States marched onward toward what was popularly perceived as its Manifest Destiny.[21]

Other capitalist connections to racism have been less direct. Capitalists, for example, have often used white racism as a strategy to maintain control over white workers and thereby keep wages low and productivity high. This has been done in two main ways. First, beginning early in the nineteenth century, there was a systematic public campaign to encourage white workers to adopt whiteness as a key part of their social identity—something they hadn't done before—and to accept the supposed superiority of whiteness as compensation for their low class position. No matter how badly treated they were by their employers, they could always look in the mirror and comfort themselves with the fact of being white and therefore elevated above people of color, even those who might have a class position higher than their own.[22] With the emancipation of the slaves following the Civil War, however, lower-class whites could no longer point to their freedom as a mark of superiority. Their response to this loss was a period of enormous violence and intimidation directed against blacks, much of which was perpetrated by the newly formed Ku Klux Klan with no serious opposition from government or the larger white population.

Another way for capitalists to control workers is to keep them worried over the possibility of losing their jobs if they demand higher wages or better working conditions. White racism has a long history of being used for this purpose. The oppressed condition of blacks and other racial minorities encourages them to work for wages that are lower than what most whites will accept. Employers have used this to pose an ongoing threat to white workers who have known employers could readily use racial minorities as an inexpensive replacement for them. This has worked most effectively as a way to break strikes and the labor unions that promote them. As unions became more powerful at the turn of the twentieth century, for example, employers often brought in black workers as strikebreakers. The strategy worked to draw the attention of white workers away from issues of capitalism and class to issues of race. It focused their fear and anger on the supposed threat from black workers, which made them less likely to see their common condition as workers and join together against the capitalists. In this way, racial division and conflict became an effective strategy for dividing different segments of the working class against one another.[23]

Similar dynamics operate today, although perhaps with greater subtlety. The controversy and conflict over affirmative action programs, for example, as well as the influx of immigrant workers from Mexico and Asia reflect an underlying belief that the greatest challenge facing white workers is unfair competition from people of color. This ignores the capitalist system itself, which by its nature increases the wealth of capitalists by controlling workers and keeping wages as low as possible, and allows a small elite to control the vast majority of wealth and income, leaving a relatively small share to be divided among everyone else. This makes for conditions of scarcity that encourage fierce competition, especially in the working and lower classes, but also in many segments of the middle class. Given the historical legacy that encourages whites to feel a sense of superiority and entitlement in relation to people of color, such competition is bound to provoke anger and resentment among whites, which is then directed at people of color rather than at those whose wealth and power lie at the heart of what is essentially an economic problem centering on the distribution of wealth. In this way, dynamics of class privilege fuel continued racism which, in turn, draws attention away from capitalism and the class oppression it produces.

Capitalism also shapes and makes use of gender inequality.[24] The cultural devaluing of women, for example, has long been used as an excuse to pay them less and exploit them as a source of cheap labor, whether in the corporate secretarial pool in New York or garment sweatshops in Los Angeles or electronics industry assembly plants in Asia.[25] Women's supposed inferiority has also been used as a basis for the belief that much of the work that women do isn't work at all and therefore isn't worthy of anything more than emotional compensation.[26] Capitalism couldn't function without the army of women who do the shopping for households (which is how most goods are purchased) and do the labor through which those goods are consumed: cooking the meals, making the bed with the new set of sheets, and so on. On a deeper level, women are, with few exceptions, the ones who nurture and raise each new generation of workers on which capitalism depends, and this vital service is provided without anyone's having to pay wages or provide health and retirement benefits. Women do it for free—even when they also work outside the home—to the benefit of the capitalist system and those who are most privileged by it.

Capitalism, then, provides an important social context for the trouble around privilege and difference. And the class dynamics that arise from capitalism interact with that trouble in powerful ways that both protect capitalism and class privilege and perpetuate privilege and oppression based on difference.

THE MATRIX OF DOMINATION AND THE PARADOX OF BEING PRIVILEGED AND UNPRIVILEGED AT THE SAME TIME

As the dynamics of capitalism and class suggest, systems of privilege are complicated. This is one reason why people can belong to a privileged category and not feel privileged. There is more than one set of categories, which means a person can belong to the privileged category in one set and an unprivileged category in another. So, for example, a middle-class white lesbian's class and race privilege may blind her to issues of race and class, or her experience of gender inequality and heterosexism may foster the illusion that this automatically prepares her to know everything she needs to know about other forms of privilege and oppression. Or a working-class white man may be annoyed by the idea that his whiteness and maleness somehow give him access to privilege. As a member of the working class, he may feel so insecure, pushed around, looked down on, and exploited that the last thing that he feels is privileged.

Part of such feelings comes from the misconception that privilege is something that is just about individuals. From that perspective, either he's privileged or he's not, just like he either has two ears or he doesn't. If he can show that he's not privileged in some way (being working-class), then that would seem to cancel out any claim that he's privileged in another.

But the truth is more complicated than whether *he* is privileged, for in a basic way, privilege isn't really about him, even though he's certainly involved in it. The social categories "white," "male," and "middle-class" are privileged in this society, and he belongs to two of those. Being working-class, however, can set up barriers that make it harder for him to attain the benefits associated with being white and male. If he can't earn a good living, for example, he may have a hard time feeling like a "real man" bonded to other men in their superiority to women. The privileged social category "male" still exists, and he belongs to it, but his social-class position gets in the way of his enjoying the advantages that go with it.

Another complication is that categories that define privilege exist all at once and in relation to one another. People never see me solely in terms of my race, for example, or my gender. Like everyone else's, my place in the social world is a package deal—white male heterosexual (middle-aged, married, father, writer, teacher, middle-class, Anglo, U.S. citizen, and on and on)—and that's the way it is all the time.

Whether, for example, my students perceive me as intelligent, credible, and competent will most likely be affected by their perception of my race. In that sense, no student could look at me simply as professor, for they will also see a person of a certain gender, race, and class. Even if they first meet me on the phone, they'll form impressions of my race if only by assuming I'm white unless I give them reason to think otherwise. In this sense, I don't exist purely as a professor separate from the other social categories I belong to.

Given that reality, it makes no sense to talk about the effect of being in one of these categories—say, white—without also looking at the others and how they're related to it. My experience of being identified as a white person in this society is affected by my also being seen as male and heterosexual and of a certain class. If I apply for a job, for example, white privilege will usually give me an edge over a similarly qualified Latino man. But if the people doing the hiring think I'm gay, my white privilege might lose out to his heterosexual privilege, and he might get the job instead of me.

It's tempting to use such comparisons to try to figure out some kind of net cost or benefit associated with each social category. In other words, you get a point for being white, male, or heterosexual, and you lose a point if you're of color, female, or homosexual. Add up the points and the result is your position in relation to systems of privilege. That would put white male heterosexuals on top (+3) and lesbians of color in some kind of "triple jeopardy" at the bottom (–3). White lesbians (–1) and gay men of color (–1) would fall somewhere in between and presumably on the same "level." This would also be true of gay white men (+1) and heterosexual white women (+1).

Life and privilege aren't that simple, however. It's not as though being male gives you a certain amount of something called "privilege" and being white gives you more of the same, and being gay cancels out half of it. Privilege takes different forms that are connected to one another in ways that aren't obvious. For example, historically one of the ways that white men have justified their domination over black men has been to portray them as sexual predators who pose a threat to white women. At the same time, they've portrayed white women as pure and needing white men's protection, a dependent position that puts them under white men's control. Notice, then, how the dynamics of gender and race are so bound up with each other that it's hard, if not impossible, to tell where one ends and the other begins. How much race or gender "counts" all by itself cannot be determined.

This is why sociologist Patricia Hill Collins describes such systems as a "matrix of domination" or what Estelle Disch calls a "matrix of privilege," and not merely a loose collection of different kinds of inequality that don't have much to do with one another. As Collins and numerous others argue, each particular form of privilege, whether based on race, gender, sexual orientation, class, religion, or ethnicity, exists only as part of a much larger system of privilege.[27]

Looking at privilege and domination in this way simplifies and clarifies things considerably. For example, once we see that each form of privilege exists only in relation to all the rest, we can stop the fruitless habit of comparing them and trying to figure out which is the worst or most oppressive.

We also free ourselves from the trap of thinking that everything is a matter of either/or—either you're oppressed or you're not, privileged or not—because reality is usually a matter of both/and. In other words, we can belong to both privileged and oppressed categories at the same time, and if we're going to make ourselves part of the solution to the problem of privilege, we have to see that. Why? Because we can't make ourselves part of the solution without seeing clearly how we're connected to the problem.

Perhaps most important, the concept of a matrix helps us see how the different dimensions of privilege and domination are connected to one another, how heterosexism is used to support male privilege, for example, or how racism is used to support class privilege. We can also see how subordinate groups are often pitted against one another in ways that draw attention away from the system of privilege that hurts them both. Asian Americans, for example, are often held up as a good example—the "model minority." This makes other racial and ethnic minorities look bad by comparison and encourages them to blame Asian Americans for their disadvantaged status.[28] In this way, Asian Americans serve as a buffer between whites and other peoples of color, as Korean Americans were in Los Angeles after the police who assaulted Rodney King were acquitted and the rage of black people spilled over into Korean neighborhoods, where stores were burned to the ground. Only when the rioting reached the edge of white neighborhoods did police finally respond to pleas for help.[29]

The complexity of the matrix of privilege and domination makes it clear that work for change needs to focus on the idea of privilege itself and all the forms it takes. We won't get rid of racism, in other words, without doing something about sexism and class, because the system that produces the one also produces the others and connects them all together.

CHAPTER 5

Making Privilege Happen

Although privilege is attached to social categories and not to individuals, people are the ones who make it happen through what they do and don't do in relation to others. This almost always involves some form of discrimination—in other words, treating people unequally simply because they belong to a particular social category.[1] Whether it's done consciously or not, discrimination has the effect of maintaining a system of privilege. Giving admissions preference to the children of graduates from elite colleges and universities, for example, is an act of discrimination because it perpetuates elite privilege by favoring their children over others regardless of their qualifications. In the same way, refusing to admit, say, Jewish students is discrimination because it perpetuates their oppressed position in relation to non-Jews.

Like all behavior, discrimination is connected to how we think and feel about people, and prejudice plays a powerful role in this.[2] Prejudice is a complicated thing, because it involves both ideas and feelings. Racial prejudice, for example, includes values that elevate whiteness above color and the belief that whites are smarter. It also includes negative feelings toward people of color—contempt, hostility, fear, disgust, and the like—along with positive (or at least neutral) feelings toward whites. Thus prejudice is a powerful force that provides fuel for discriminatory behavior and a rationale for justifying it.

Privilege, then, is something that happens through what people think and feel and do, and it takes many active forms, from overt hostility to the subtlety of looking away.[3] It works at every level, from the spirit and the body to having a decent place to live and enough food to eat. As sociologists Joe Feagin and Melvin Sikes point out in their book *Living with Racism,* the consequences of privilege must be understood as lived experience that both damages people in the moment and accumulates over time to affect not only their behavior, but also their understanding of themselves and life itself.[4] And no matter what form privilege takes, it involves everyone in one way or another.

AVOIDANCE, EXCLUSION, REJECTION, AND WORSE

Of all human needs, few are as powerful as the need to be seen, included, and accepted by other people. This is why being shunned or banished is among the most painful punishments to endure, a social death. It's not surprising, then, that inclusion and acceptance are used as a basis for privilege. To see how, consider all the choices people can make that affect whether other people feel welcome and valued or like outsiders who don't belong:

- Whether we look at people when we talk with them.
- Whether we smile at people when they walk into the room, or stare as if to say, "What are *you* doing here?" or stop the conversation with a hush they have to wade through to be included in the smallest way.

- Whether we listen and respond to what people say, or drift away to someone or something else; whether we talk about things they know about, or stick to what's peculiar to the "in-group."

- Whether we acknowledge that diversity exists and make room for it, or act as though everyone is either like us or, by default, *should* be like us.

- Whether we acknowledge people's presence, or make them wait as if they weren't there; whether we avoid touching their skin when giving or taking something; how closely we watch them to see what they're up to.

- Whether we avoid someone walking down the street, giving them a wide berth when we pass or even crossing to the other side.

- Whether we share with new colleagues the informal rules that you have to know to succeed, belong, or get along—or turn the conversation to something light and superficial when they're around.

- Whether we invite people to our home or out for a drink and talk.

- Whether we say hello to people when they move into the neighborhood.

Avoidance, exclusion, rejection, and devaluing often happen in ways noticed only by the person experiencing them, and can happen without anyone's intending harm. It can be as subtle as shifting your gaze, leaning your body away, or editing your speech. It can be faint praise ("Uh-huh, okay"), or praise that's so effusive ("Wow, you're really articulate!"), it signals surprise at the person's having exceeded low expectations. It can be repeatedly asking someone if they understand what you've said, as if they're too stupid to have gotten it the first time. It can be using images of darkness and blackness as negative, and whiteness as positive, or using "queer" or "gay" as insults, or "having balls" (but not

ovaries) as a metaphor for courage. It can be paying more attention to a woman's looks than to her ability or character, and
encouraging her to do the same. It can be as unmindful as treating all people as though they were Christian ("Merry Christ-
mas!") or heterosexual ("Feel free to bring your spouse."). It can
be as simple as not paying attention, as when elegantly dressed
black presidential candidate Jesse Jackson was tipped by a white
woman who confused him with a bellboy who'd just helped her
in a New York hotel.[5] It can be telling what seems to be a joke,
but in fact signals the low esteem in which people are held simply
because they're female or gay or a race other than white.

To look at racism in particular, as subtle as it often is, racism
also happens openly and on purpose. It appears in swastikas and
racial epithets scrawled on college dormitory walls, in Asian
American students' being spat upon as they walk across campus
or receiving hate e-mail. It appears in crosses burned on front
lawns of African Americans who've just moved into a neighborhood, and in churches and synagogues burned to the ground
and graveyards strewn with toppled tombstones.

It happens when real estate agents steer people of color
away from white neighborhoods and bank officers deny them
mortgages and business loans readily granted to whites who are
no more qualified than they are. As a result, blacks are the most
residentially segregated group in America. The consequences
are almost incalculable, for study after study shows that geo-
graphic mobility is a key to social mobility and improved quality
of life. Where people live, for example, makes a huge difference
in the jobs they have access to, the quality of community services
(schools, health care, street maintenance, trash disposal), and
their ability to affect those who govern them.[6]

Racism comes out in police harassment, brutality, and
neglect in moments of crisis; in being pulled over and having
your car searched for a "DWB" ("Driving While Black") viola-
tion. It comes out in black parents' having to train their teenage

sons to avoid the police at all costs, to never run away from them if they do encounter them, to keep their hands out in the open, to never give cause for suspicion—in other words, to never act like a child moving through the world freely and without fear. It comes out in "nigger" muttered in passing on a crowded sidewalk or scrawled on public bathroom walls; in billboard advertising campaigns for cigarettes and alcohol that target lower- and working-class African American neighborhoods. It comes out in vacant apartments that suddenly become unavailable, in hotel reservations that are mysteriously "lost" when a person of color arrives to claim them.

For African Americans, the result is a daily grind of always feeling vulnerable to judgments based solely on their race, because mistakes and failure are never just that, but always carry the potential to "confirm the broader, racial inferiority they are suspected of."[7] Racism means living in a society that predisposes whites to see the worst in them and ignore the best, a society where acceptance must be won anew every day. It means having to carry a continuing "minority sense," a "race watch" for the possibility of hostility, and a "second eye" to decide whether to give whites the benefit of the doubt.[8]

"It is utterly exhausting being Black in America," writes the children's advocate Marian Wright Edelman, who is black, "physically, mentally, and emotionally. . . . There is no respite from your badge of color."[9]

It is, as a black college professor put it, to lead "lives of quiet desperation generated by a litany of *daily* large and small events that, whether or not by design, remind us of our 'place' in American society."[10] It is to experience a precarious balance between paranoia and the desire to live life simply as it comes, an endless struggle with humiliation, depression, and rage.

Racism, of course, isn't the only form of exclusion and oppression. An ongoing epidemic of violence threatens women and gay men, at home and at work and on the street. A majority of girls and women in U.S. schools and workplaces report being sexually harassed; domestic violence is a leading cause of injury to women; almost half of all the females born in the United States can expect to experience an attempted or completed rape sometime during their lives.[11] The result is patterns of chronic fear and avoidance as women and girls learn to circumscribe their lives in order to reduce the odds of being singled out for harassment or attack.

When subordinate groups get fed up and speak out about their rage, frustration, and resentment, there's always the danger that powerful others—men, whites, Anglos, heterosexuals, the middle and upper classes—won't like what they hear and will retaliate with the epithets "unprofessional," "malcontent," "maladjusted," "whiner," "too emotional," "bitch," "out of control," "male-basher."[12] Given the cultural authority and the power to harm that such retaliation carries, there isn't a lot that people can do to defend themselves against it.

The problem of privilege infects both our outer and inner lives and flows between them in ways that intensify and perpetuate both. It appears in unequal distributions of income and wealth that grow worse as competition intensifies over jobs that pay a living wage and as the concentration of wealth and power in corporations and the upper classes expands in the global economy. It appears in unequal treatment, access, and opportunities in education, work, health care, and the courts, and in severe underrepresentation in every major organization from religious to corporate to political.

At work, the effects of privilege show up in glass ceilings and occupational ghettos. Asian Americans, for example, are routinely treated like "techno-coolies" to be managed for their talents but never allowed to manage themselves or others,[13] and to be channeled into narrow technical specialties and then envied and resented when they excel at them.

Jobs are so segregated by gender that half of all workers would have to change occupations in order for women and men to be equally represented across the U.S. economy. The dynamics of privilege are also reflected in upper-level jobs like "community relations" that for all their apparent trappings of success are often dead-end pedestals for displaying—and containing—minority tokens; or in women and racial minorities who don't get mentored and whose potential and accomplishments are all but invisible. Blacks and Latinos, for example, are significantly underrepresented in managerial and professional occupations, often averaging only a half to two-thirds of their proportional share of the employed labor force. They are significantly *over*represented in clerical and support occupations, government jobs such as mail carriers, and lower-level service and blue-collar jobs.[14]

And while education certainly helps, in many ways it doesn't help much. African Americans and Latinos with four or more years of college are, respectively, 78 and 61 percent more likely to be unemployed than comparable whites; and African American and Latino families with college-educated householders are two to three times more likely than similar white families to live below the poverty line.[15] Similar dynamics work in regard to gender inequality. Although the gender gap in income has shrunk somewhat over the past several decades, the pace is extremely slow. Women college graduates who worked full time and year-round earned an average of $17,000 in 1982 compared with $28,000 for men, a ratio of 62 cents to the dollar. By 1998, the comparable averages had risen to $39,655 for women and $60,605 for men, for a ratio of 65 cents to the dollar, increasing at a rate of a penny every six years.[16]

In all its forms, the problem of privilege and oppression stands between us and the kind of world in which all people have the best chance of thriving. To do something about it, we first have to see how it affects us, because only then are we likely to feel a personal obligation to act.

A PROBLEM FOR WHOM?

No matter where we look—and for all the complaints and controversy about affirmative action—the position of dominant groups shows little sign of weakening. For all that, however, the people who belong to them don't escape the negative consequences of privilege. Consider, for example, the impoverishment of men's lives caused by the culturally encouraged emotional gulfs between them and their fathers, sons, and male friends. Consider the damage men often do to themselves and one another in trying to measure up as "real men," how they limit their humanity, deny their needs, don't ask for help, and live with chronic fear, anxiety, isolation, and loneliness. Consider men's fear of other men's violence and aggression, and boys who feel driven to shoot down classmates and teachers. Consider the difficulty of true cross-gender friendship and in men's predictable defensiveness around women—men feel vulnerable to accusations of sexism or harassment in a world organized to privilege them at women's expense. Consider the range of reactions to the most subtle mention of male privilege: hypersensitive, huffy, hurt, worried, hostile, confused, shut down, tuned out, unable to "get it," rushing to backpedal, dismiss, counter, refute, condescend, patronize, trivialize, ridicule, or just walk away.

The disadvantages of male privilege are similar to those of heterosexual privilege. By definition, gay men and lesbians bear the brunt of heterosexism and homophobia.[17] But the dynamic that harms them also has destructive effects on heterosexuals. In the simplest sense, weapons used against homosexuals are also used among heterosexuals, especially among men. Power plays a key role in gender dynamics, especially in patterns of gender inequality. But it also looms large in men's competition with other men—the jockeying for status and trying to measure up to mainstream standards of masculinity. As part of this dynamic, the same insults and intimidation that heterosexual men use against gay men—"fag," "queer," "fairy," "cocksucker"—they also routinely use against other heterosexual men to enhance their status. Sometimes such homosexual tags are used openly; at other times the message is coded in words such as "wimp," "wuss," or "whipped." In either case, whenever a man's manhood is challenged, his vulnerability to being tarred with cultural references to being gay is never far off, regardless of whether his sexual orientation is truly in doubt. Similar dynamics operate to keep women in line. Lesbian-baiting is a powerful way to intimidate all women into silence on gender issues for fear of being tagged as lesbians.[18]

This particular gender dynamic among men gives only a hint of the trouble heterosexuals are in. Consider the enormous amount of male aggression, violence, and harassment directed at girls and women, from child sexual abuse to battering, rape, and sexual harassment.[19] Studies of male violence show that control is a core issue, especially through the cultural connection between power ("potency") and heterosexual relationships. A real man is defined as one who is always in control, and sexuality is identified as a major way for men to prove it. Since violence is primarily a means for exerting control and asserting superiority, the cultural association between heterosexuality and male power actually promotes male violence against women in heterosexual relationships.

Because heterosexuality plays such a large part in defining gender inequality—"real" men and women are always defined in heterosexual terms—gender violence often has a sexual aspect to it. As a result, the violence inflicted on lesbians and gay men by heterosexual men and the violence among heterosexual couples are deeply related to each other.[20] Most heterosexual men who attack lesbians and gay men do so not because of moral or religious conviction, but because they feel threatened and

uneasy over the mere existence of people whose sexual orientation and relation to women raise questions about their own.
Since lesbians and gay men don't follow heterosexual models,
the example they set challenges heterosexual men's claim to
a monopoly over "real manhood," especially as measured by
power over women. Gay men challenge the dominant masculine
model by not relating to women as objects of sexual power. Lesbians challenge it by not choosing or submitting to men as sexual partners. This makes it hard to separate the dynamics of
gender inequality in heterosexual relationships and the trouble
heterosexuals make for homosexuals.

Just as there is gender trouble for men and heterosexist
trouble for heterosexuals, there is also race trouble for whites. It
shows up in all the things white people do to get around the fact
that the enormous suffering caused by racism has something to
do with the social status of being white, no matter how whites
see themselves as individuals.[21] It is reflected in discomfort and
fear around blacks, in demonizing black men and boys, in
hypersensitive defensiveness around issues of race.[22] You can
see the race trouble for whites in the uneasy feeling they get
when they realize they aren't trusted and realize they're being
told what they want to hear rather than the truth. You can see it
in how white people deaden themselves against the pain they'd
feel if they realized how deeply racism compromises their own
lives, how much it deadens the spirit and flattens the emotional
landscape, how it sets whites up to look at the "rhythm" and
"life" in non-European cultures with the nagging feeling of
something lacking in their own.

You can see the race trouble for whites in the toll it takes on
moral integrity: racism naturally requires hypocrisy toward some
of the most deeply held cultural values of fairness, decency, and
justice. You can see it in the lengths to which white people will
go to distort current and historical reality in order to maintain
the illusion of being the chosen and superior race, the standard

against which others are to be measured. You can see it in how poorly prepared white people are to be effective on a global scale, where whites are, for all their power, a small and shrinking minority. You can see it in the angry, wishful naïveté of "I don't see color; I don't see race." You can see it in the pointed ignoring of the "deceptively comfortable prison" of racism that white people live in and the chronic fear that "the murky waters of despair and dread that now flood the streets of black America" will touch them, too, if not sweep them and everything they cherish away.[23]

But the trouble of race already touches them. White people are up to their necks in it just by being here.

What we don't realize most of the time is that the "isms"—sexism, heterosexism, racism—affect more than women, homosexuals, and racial and ethnic minorities. They affect everyone, because it's impossible to live in a world that generates so much trouble, injustice, and suffering without being touched by it. Everyone has a race, a gender, a sexual orientation, and an ethnic background. Whether we like it or not, we all figure in the differences that the trouble around difference is about. The bad news is that no matter who you are, the trouble is *your* trouble. But that's also the good news, because it also gives you the potential and a reason to do something about it.

AND THAT'S NOT ALL

In addition to how it affects people, the trouble around difference also affects organizations, communities, and society as a whole. In corporations and the military and neighborhood schools, the prevalence of racism, sexism, and heterosexism is among our worst-kept secrets. Much of the time, people manage to act as though nothing's wrong—and then another scandal explodes onto the front pages: racist talk and behavior at the highest levels of responsibility and power; Matthew Shepard, a young man tortured and murdered in 1998 because of his sexual orientation; sexual violence and harassment treated as routine and unremarkable by companies as prominent as Ford Motor Company until someone makes an issue of it; hate crimes in the halls of colleges and universities, institutions that present themselves as sanctuaries for enlightenment and reason.

Most organizations either deny the trouble or are oblivious to it. When a crisis breaks through the routine of business as usual, the typical reaction is panicked efforts at damage control to minimize legal exposure and bad publicity. Invariably, the attention goes to a few misbehaving individuals, in the belief that getting rid of or fixing them or learning how to spot them before they do something wrong is enough to take care of the problem.

Between crises and scandals, privilege continues its insidious work of making organizations increasingly dysfunctional and vulnerable. It makes it all but impossible, for example, for white male managers and teachers to effectively mentor white women and people of color—if they even try in the first place, which they usually don't. White men's position in the world gives them few ways to know what their female and minority students and junior colleagues are up against as they try to move upward in organizations. White men also see little reason to examine themselves in relation to the racism and sexism that haunt so many people's lives, to come to terms with how living in a racist and sexist world has shaped them and how they see other people and themselves. They might try to be fair, which is to say, to treat racial minorities as they would whites, or women as they would men. But this approach pretends that racism and sexism don't exist beyond their personal intentions. This makes it easier for them to feel unconnected to the trouble, but it doesn't serve the needs of people on the outside looking in.

Privilege and oppression are the proverbial elephant in the room, and if the teacher or the boss won't talk about it, the subordinate trying to learn the ropes and get ahead certainly won't take the risk of making powerful people uncomfortable by bringing it up. With so much of importance left unsaid and such crucial issues left untouched, it's hard to trust those in power—and, on some level, there's good reason not to. As a result, people don't learn what they need to know in order to succeed. They wind up stuck in place, or in some backwater position within the organization, their talents and abilities unrealized and of no particular use to anyone, including themselves. Or they strike out on their own, dropping out of school or transferring to another university, for example, or leaving a job to start their own business or to work for a company that understands the importance of meeting the issue head-on.

For the organizations that are left behind, their investment in training and development is lost, and the word goes out that if you aren't white, aren't heterosexual, aren't male, and aren't desperate, you'll do better someplace else, someplace where you can look at those with power and influence and see people who look like you. And as competition intensifies and the population of students and workers diversifies, those "someplace elses" wind up doing better because they attract and keep talent that comes in all kinds of people.

Most organizations' failure in the area of diversity occurs not because they're run by mean-spirited white male bigots— few are—but because they deal with diversity badly or not at all, unless a crisis forces the issue. Even then, they deal with it only enough to make it seem to go away, which usually doesn't include confronting the reality of privilege and oppression.

The failure doesn't happen all at once in some dramatic moment of truth. The splashy scandals—the inflammatory incident, the raving bigot found out, the harassing professor unmasked—aren't the problem. The problem is the same culture of denial and neglect that permeates society as a whole. Little by little, day by day, the struggle to earn a living or a degree and maintain a sense of dignity and self-worth in the face of one sign after another that they don't really matter or belong wears people down, sapping morale and draining talent.

The oppressive effect of privilege is often so insidious that dominant groups complain whenever it's brought up for discussion. They feel impatient and imposed upon. "Come on," they say, "stop whining. Things aren't that bad. Maybe they used to be, but not anymore. It's time to move on. Get over it." But people who are white or heterosexual or male or middle- or upper-class have to ask themselves how they would *know* how bad it really is to be a person of color or lesbian or a woman or gay or working or lower class. What life experience, for example, would qualify a white person to know the day-to-day reality of racism? People of color are, by comparison, experts in the dynamics of race privilege, because they live with the oppressive consequences of it twenty-four hours a day. White people simply do not. Whites may know what it's like to get bad service in a restaurant, for example, but they have no idea what it's like to get bad service so often—and to have it happen to all of their friends and relations—that they can't escape the reality that it's tied to how people see them as a human being simply because of their race.[24]

None of this means that everything racial and ethnic minorities or women or homosexuals say is true. But it does mean there's every reason for members of dominant groups to give them the benefit of the doubt long enough to look at the issues they're talking about.

WE CAN'T HEAL UNTIL
THE WOUNDING STOPS

There is a lot of talk these days about "racial healing," healing "gender wounds," and "reconciliation" of various kinds. These are powerful and inspiring images that carry the promise of a soothing end to a difficult and destructive time in U.S. history. The war is over, the damage done. Now we can turn to the difficult but ultimately triumphant work of undoing the damage and healing the wounds inflicted upon us individually and collectively.

If true, this would be a blessing, but in fact it is wishful thinking. Problems of privilege and oppression are far from over. Every day they damage tens of millions of people. The patterns of history continue into the present and show every sign of going on into the future unless people do something to change them. And the only way to do that is to change the role they play in making privilege happen.

Healing imagery is also problematic because it implies that the damage being done is primarily emotional. The goal becomes one of "getting along" better by being nicer and more tolerant toward one another, forgiving and forgetting, living in more authentic ways. I don't object to this goal, but it ignores the fact that a lot of the trouble doesn't begin and end with interpersonal relations and emotional wounds. Much of it is embedded in structures of power and inequality that shape almost every aspect of life in this society, from economics to politics to religion to schools and the family. The idea that we're going to get out of this by somehow getting to a place where we're kinder and more sensitive to one another ignores most of what we have to overcome. It sets us up to walk right past the trouble toward an alternative that doesn't exist and can't exist until we do something about what creates privilege and oppression in the first place, and that is something that needs to be changed, not healed.

In some ways, appeals to healing turn out to be—in effect if not intent—another way to deny the depth of the trouble we're in. They feed on the desperate and powerful illusion that if we ignore it long enough, or try to replace it with good intentions, it will go away. But the hope for something better depends on the ability to work together to face that illusion and go through it to the truth on the other side. To do that, we first have to understand how the trouble around difference is made worse by how we think about it—the trouble we have with the trouble.

CHAPTER 6

The Trouble with the Trouble

I am in a three-day meeting of human resource managers. It is one of the most diverse groups I've ever seen—roughly half women and half men, half white and half black, and from all over the United States as well as a dozen European countries. They share a deep and in many cases lifelong commitment to ending oppression. Individually and collectively, they're responsible for some of the best diversity success stories large organizations have to tell.

As I listen to them talk about their work, it's obvious how frustrated they are in spite of all they've accomplished. Progress is painfully slow and easily undone when leadership changes or a budget crunch dries up resources needed to carry the work forward. But the malaise goes deeper than that to the horns of a dilemma that emerges as the day wears on. They know that the only way to deal effectively with these issues is to engage managers and vice presidents who have the power to shape organizational culture and set examples that bring others along. They also know that "manager" or "vice president" usually means "white heterosexual male," because that's who the overwhelming majority of people in control of large organizations are, whether it's universities, unions, government, churches, professional sports, or the mass media.

Everyone in the room knows that the key is to engage members of dominant groups with issues of difference and privilege as an ongoing, permanent part of their lives. In other words, privilege has to be as much an issue for them as it is for women, racial minorities, lesbians, gay men, poor people, and others who bear the brunt of the oppression it causes in everyday life.

In other words, if dominant groups *really* saw privilege and oppression as unacceptable—if white people saw race as *their* issue, if men saw gender as a *men's* issue, if heterosexuals saw heterosexism as *their* problem—privilege and oppression wouldn't have much of a future. But this isn't what's happening. Dominant groups *don't* engage with these issues, and when they do, it's not for long or with much effect.

I ask the human resource managers "Why not?" and the response pours out of them without hesitation. Dominant groups don't see privilege as a problem

■ *Because they don't know it exists in the first place.* They're oblivious to it. The reality of privilege doesn't occur to them because they don't go out of their way to see it or ask about it and because no one dares bring it up for fear of making things worse. Dominant groups have no idea of how their privilege oppresses others. This obliviousness allows them to cruise along and tend to the details of their own lives (which are, of course, considerable, just like everyone else's), with only an occasional sense of trouble somewhere "out there" just beyond the fringe of their consciousness. This lack of awareness also gives them a low tolerance for hearing about the trouble, for when the normal state of affairs is silence, any mention of it feels like an imposition.[1]

■ *Because they don't have to.* If you point it out to them, they may acknowledge that the trouble exists. Otherwise, they don't pay attention, because privilege insulates them from its consequences. There is nothing to compel their attention except, perhaps, when a schoolyard shooting or a sexual harassment lawsuit or a race riot or an O.J. Simpson trial disrupts the usual flow of things.

■ *Because they think it's just a personal problem.* They think individuals usually get what they deserve, which makes the trouble just a sum of individual troubles. This means that if whites or males get more than others, it's because they have it coming—they work harder, they're smarter, more capable. If other people get less, it's up to them to do something about it.

■ *Because they want to hang on to their privilege.* On some level, they know they benefit from the status quo and they don't want that to change. Some people have mixed feelings, such as a white man who said in a workshop that he felt "torn between wanting to make things right and not wanting to lose what I have." Many others, however, feel a sense of entitlement, that they deserve everything they have, including whatever advantages they have over others. As one male student at a university in Colorado said to me recently, "Why should men's athletic programs have to give up any funding to women? If they want more money for their programs, let them go find it." Such feelings can be especially powerful among those whose lack of class privilege leads them to deny the very existence of gender, race, and other forms of privilege that advantage them. For them, resistance to change isn't about hanging on to privilege because they don't experience themselves as having any. Instead, they see themselves as struggling to succeed in a system that is based on competition and scarcity, and reluctant to give up anything that lends them an edge. Similar dynamics can sometimes appear among those who are privileged by their class position. I once worked with a group of highly successful white professional women, for example, who became furious when we pressed them on issues of race. They were happy to talk about male privilege and how it frustrated their upward mobility, but wanted no part of the idea that privilege attached to their own whiteness was something they needed to look at.

- *Because they're prejudiced—racist, sexist, heterosexist, classist.* They're consciously hostile toward blacks, women, lesbians, gay men, the poor. They believe in the superiority of their group, and the belief is like a high, thick wall. The more you try to get through it or over it, the higher and thicker it gets. They're the white executives who talk in racist ways in the privacy of their offices, the Army drill sergeants who sexually assault female trainees, the professors who harass female students by pressuring them for sex or holding them up for ridicule in their classes, the middle-class people who look the other way when they pass a homeless person on the street, or a presidential candidate who vows not to appoint gay or lesbian Cabinet secretaries.

- *Because they're afraid.* They may be sympathetic to doing something about the trouble, but they're afraid of being blamed for it if they acknowledge that it exists. They're afraid of being saddled with guilt just for being white or male or middle-class, attacked with no place to hide. They're even more afraid that members of their own group—other whites, other heterosexuals, other men— will reject them if they break ranks and call attention to issues of privilege, making people feel uncomfortable or threatened. Since even these beneficiaries of privilege are often worried and frightened already about so many things in their lives—such as losing their jobs or being passed over for promotion—this challenge appears as just one more thing to be afraid of.

These reasons don't apply to everyone in the same way or to the same degree, in part because "they" aren't a homogeneous collection of people. As we've seen, privilege is complicated, and each of its various dimensions—race, ethnicity, gender, class, sexual orientation—affects how people deal with its other dimensions.

Regardless of such variations and exceptions, if members of dominant groups pay attention to privilege and oppression, it's always in spite of the many reasons not to. Dealing with those reasons brings us to the core dilemma around diversity.

The roomful of human resources managers were responsible for success stories in raising diversity consciousness in organizations. Why, then, were they so frustrated and so painfully aware of things *not* working for change? As I listened to them, I realized the progress they've made has depended on two strategies that are effective, but only to a limited degree and, even then, just in the short run. Because they see these as their only alternatives, they feel stuck.

The first strategy is to appeal to privileged people's sense of decency and fairness, their good will toward those less fortunate than themselves, what one manager calls the "tin cup" approach. "Help us do something about these issues," the pitch goes, "because it's the right thing, the moral, good, noble thing to do."

The tin cup touches many people and sometimes even moves them to action, but as a strategy for long-term change, it fails for several reasons. It depends on an impulse of generosity toward others, and this impulse tends to rise and fall depending on how secure the privileged feel in their own situations. This is why even the most progressive organizations will support diversity work when their bottom line is healthy and cut back at the first sign of hard times (in the same way that public schools cut back on art, music, and other "expressive" programs when money gets tight).

The do-the-right-thing approach also rests on a sense of "us" and "them"—the "us" who help and the less fortunate "them" who get helped. The problem is that the former feel very little reason to identify with the latter. When "we" who are not poor or of color, for example, help out "those people" who are poor or of color, there can be a real separation and distance even at the moment of reaching out to help. In fact, the act of helping—of being able to help—can reaffirm the social distance between the two groups and heighten everyone's awareness of it. Thus every act of giving to others is always a statement, intended or not, of one group's ability to give and the other's inability to get along without it. And in a society that counts independence, autonomy, and self-sufficiency among its highest cultural values, it's impossible to avoid the negative judgments attached to those on the receiving end and the status-enhancing judgments conferred on those who give.

Although doing the right thing can be morally compelling, it usually rests on a sense of obligation to principle more than to people, which can lead to disconnection rather than connection. I take care of my children, for example, not because it's the right thing to do and the neighbors would disapprove if I didn't, but because I feel a sense of connection to them that carries with it an automatic sense of responsibility for their welfare. The less connected to them I feel, the less responsible I'll feel. It isn't that I *owe* them something as a debtor owes a creditor; it's rather that my life is bound up in their lives and theirs in mine, which means that what happens to them in a sense also happens to me. I don't experience them as "others" whom I decide to help because it's the right thing to do and I'm feeling charitable at the moment. The family is something larger than myself that I participate in, and I can't be part of that without paying attention to what goes on in it.

Another problem with acting merely from a sense of principle is that part of its appeal is the good feeling it gives people about themselves when they do it, which can motivate them only in the short run. Confronting issues like sexism and racism is hard and sometimes painful and even frightening work, and feeling good about being virtuous isn't likely to sustain people over the rugged course of it.

What can sustain them is a sense of *ownership,* that the trouble is truly *their* trouble and not someone else's, because this means that their responsibility to do something no longer feels like an option. It isn't something they can choose to do if they're in a generous mood or can "afford" to at the moment. It is, quite simply, one of the terms of their participation in the world they live in, however large or small they define it to be. Without that sense of ownership, serious work on issues of privilege will always be what Roosevelt Thomas calls a "fair weather" item on the agenda.[2]

Thomas urges us to follow an alternative to the tin cup approach. We should do something about privilege and oppression, he tells us, not because it's the socially responsible, right thing to do, but because it makes organizations work better. It helps businesses compete for customers and the best employees and universities compete for the best students and staff. It raises morale and productivity and lowers costly turnovers. It protects against lawsuits and all the energy that goes into worrying about them.

In an important sense, of course, he's right: for corporations and universities, the "business case" for dealing with the trouble around privilege is a compelling one. It underlies the most successful corporate initiatives at companies like Dow Corning and Avon. When women and racial minorities leave unsupportive workplaces and take their training and talent with them, the annual loss to organizations can run into millions of dollars. That's far more than it would cost to fund programs to improve the conditions that prompt people to leave. When you factor in the other costs and liabilities that result from an unsupportive or hostile environment, you'd think organizations would fall all over themselves in the rush to do something about it.

But most of the time they don't, and when they do, it often comes across as a halfhearted, short-lived, "flavor of the month" program that can leave people feeling cynical and, having had their expectations raised and dashed, even worse than before. ("It pisses me off," said a woman line supervisor at one of the largest U.S. manufacturers, "that they're doing this just to make a buck.") Or the program is serious and intense, but lacks follow-up or fades away when key people leave or budgets are cut. The problem with relying on the business case is that it sees ending the trouble as a means to an end, a practical, rational strategy. Thus it's only as good as the results it produces in comparison with alternative strategies. If a more "efficient" way can be found to improve the bottom line or protect against losses—especially in the short run—then it's likely to replace the diversity strategy.

This is why the business case, for all its surface validity, cannot be the *only* basis for action. At the right moment, the business case can appeal to fear or greed or both, but as anyone knows who watches the ups and downs of the stock market, fear is something that comes and goes, and greed easily attaches itself to whatever looks good at the moment. This is especially true in the short run, which is increasingly the perspective of choice in a competitive and insecure capitalist world.

Short-run thinking encourages organizations to act like Hindus in India who make the mistake of eating their cows during droughts when food is in short supply. Cows are vital to Indian agriculture. They serve as draft animals in rice fields (their cloven hooves don't get stuck in the muck), and their dung is used for everything from building blocks to fuel. In the middle of a famine, a cow can look awfully good as a short-run solution to hunger. But giving in to the temptation leads to long-run disaster: when the rains return, you can't raise any crops because you've eaten your most important farming resource. Anthropologist Marvin Harris argues that this is why the cow became a sacred symbol in the Hindu religion—it was the only way powerful enough to keep people from eating their cows when the temptation was the greatest.[3]

Organizations that ignore issues of privilege and oppression are in effect eating their cows by focusing only on short-run consequences. When push comes to shove and they need all the talent and commitment they can get in a highly competitive world, it simply won't be there. The human potential that comes in packages that don't qualify as white or male or heterosexual or European will be long gone, fled across the street to competitors willing to confront these issues and do something about them.

Certainly life would be better in a world without racism and sexism and other forms of oppression. Surely removing the resentment, fear, injustice, and suffering that go with them would dramatically improve life in schools, workplaces, neighborhoods, and communities. Short-run competitive thinking, however, makes that goal all but impossible to achieve, because effecting that kind of change is inherently a long-term project. Even when people can see the benefits somewhere off in the distance, they still need something to hold them to the vision and see them through the long journey from here to there. Appealing to lofty principles or the bottom line can't do it, because those approaches too easily give way to forces and considerations that are powerful in the short run even if they're disastrous in the long run.

What's needed is a sense of ownership in relation to the problem and the path people need to walk toward its solution. What's needed is some reason to feel committed to change that's powerful enough to win out against all the reasons dominant groups have to turn away and leave it to someone else: the anger, fear, resentment, detachment, inattention, ignorance, and the luxury of obliviousness. The personal stake in issues of privilege runs deeper than that, to the realization that everyone is connected to a great deal of suffering in the world, and anyone who allows awareness of that to enter their consciousness is bound to feel something about it.

We need a third choice, one that can take us beyond simple appeals to goodness or enhancing the bottom line. We need a way to remove the barriers that keep well-intentioned members of dominant groups stuck in a place where they don't see themselves as part of the solution. We need a way to have serious conversations across difference, and to *act* across difference toward ending the most damaging source of unnecessary suffering in the human experience.

CHAPTER 7

Privilege, Power,
Difference, and Us

To do something about the trouble around difference, we
have to talk about it, but most of the time we don't, because
it feels too risky. This is true for just about everyone, but especially for members of privileged categories, for whites, for men,
and for heterosexuals. As Paul Kivel writes, for example, "Rarely
do we whites sit back and listen to people of color without interrupting, without being defensive, without trying to regain attention to ourselves, without criticizing or judging."[1]

The discomfort, defensiveness, and fear come in part from
not knowing how to talk about privilege without feeling vulnerable to anger and blame. They will continue until we find a way to
reduce the risk of talking about privilege. The key to reducing
the risk lies in understanding what makes talking about privilege
seem so risky. I don't mean that risk is an illusion. There is no
way to do this work without the possibility that people will feel
uncomfortable or frightened or threatened. But the risk isn't
nearly as big as it seems, for like the proverbial (and mythical)

human fear of the strange and unfamiliar, the problem begins with how people *think* about things and who they are in relation to them.

INDIVIDUALISM: OR, THE MYTH THAT EVERYTHING IS SOMEBODY'S FAULT

We live in a society that encourages us to think that the social world begins and ends with individuals. It's as if an organization or a society is just a collection of people, and everything that happens in it begins with what they each think, feel, and intend. If you understand people, the reasoning goes, then you also understand social life. It's an appealing way to think, because it's grounded in our experience as individuals, which is what we know best. But it's also misleading, because it boxes us into a narrow and distorted view of reality. In other words, it isn't true.

If we use individualism to explain sexism, for example, it's hard to avoid the idea that sexism exists simply because men *are* sexist—men have sexist feelings, beliefs, needs, and motivations that lead them to behave in sexist ways. If sexism produces evil consequences, it's because men *are* evil, hostile, and malevolent toward women. In short, everything bad in the world is seen as somebody's fault, which is why talk about privilege so often turns into a game of hot potato.

Individualistic thinking keeps us stuck in the trouble by making it almost impossible to talk seriously about it. It encourages women, for example, to blame and distrust men. It sets men up to feel personally attacked if anyone mentions gender issues, and to define those issues as a "women's problem." It also encourages men who don't think or behave in overtly sexist ways—the ones most likely to become part of the solution—to conclude that sexism has nothing to do with them, that it's just a problem for "bad" men. The result is a kind of paralysis: people either talk about sexism in the most superficial, unthreatening, trivializing, and even stupid way ("The Battle of the Sexes," *Men Are from Mars, Women Are from Venus*), or they don't talk about it at all.[2]

Breaking the paralysis begins with realizing that the social world consists of a lot more than individuals. We are always participating in something larger than ourselves—what sociologists call social systems—and systems are more than collections of people. A university, for example, is a social system, and people participate in it. But the people aren't the university and the university isn't the people. This means that to understand what happens in it, we have to look at both the university and how individual people participate in it. If patterns of racism exist in a society, for example, the reason is never just a matter of white people's personalities, feelings, or intentions. We also have to understand how they participate in particular kinds of social systems, how this participation shapes their behavior, and what consequences it produces.

INDIVIDUALS, SYSTEMS, AND PATHS OF LEAST RESISTANCE

To see the difference between a system and the people who participate in it, consider a game like Monopoly. I used to play Monopoly, but I don't anymore because I don't like the way I behave when I do. Like everyone else, as a Monopoly player I try to take everything from the other players—all their money, all their property—which then forces them out of the game. The point of the game is to ruin everyone else and be the only one left in the end. When you win, you feel good, because you're *supposed* to feel good. Except that one day I realized that I felt good about winning—about taking everything from everyone else—even when I played with my children, who were pretty young at the time. But there didn't seem to be much point to playing without trying to win, because winning is what the game is *about*. Why land on a property and not buy it, or own a property and not improve it, or have other players land on your property and not collect the rent? So I stopped playing.

And it worked, because the fact is that I don't behave in such greedy ways when I'm not playing Monopoly, even though it's still me, Allan, in either case. So what's all this greedy behavior about? Do we behave in greedy ways simply because we *are* greedy? In a sense, the answer is yes in that greed is part of the human repertoire of possible motivations, just like compassion, altruism, or fear. But how, then, do I explain the absence of such behavior when I'm not playing Monopoly? Clearly, the answer has to include both me as an individual human being who's capable of making all kinds of choices *and* something about the social situation in which I make those choices. It's not one or the other; it's both in relation to each other.

If we think of Monopoly as a social system—as "something larger than ourselves that we participate in"—then we can see how people and systems come together in a dynamic relationship that produces the patterns of social life, including problems around difference and privilege. People are indisputably the ones who make social systems happen. If no one plays Monopoly, it's just a box full of stuff with writing inside the cover. When people open it up and identify themselves as players, however, Monopoly starts to *happen*. This makes people very important, but we shouldn't confuse that with Monopoly itself. We aren't Monopoly and Monopoly isn't us. I can describe the game and how it works without saying anything about the personal characteristics of all the people who play it or might play it.

People make Monopoly happen, but *how?* How do we know what to do? How do we choose from the millions of things that, as human beings, we *could* do at any given moment? The answer is the other half of the dynamic relation between individuals and systems. As we sit around the table, we make Monopoly happen from one minute to the next. But our participation in the game also shapes how *we* happen as people—what we think and feel and do. This doesn't mean that systems control us in a rigid and predictable way. Instead, systems load the odds in certain directions by offering what I call "paths of least resistance" for us to follow.

In every social situation, we have an almost limitless number of choices we might make. Sitting in a movie theater, for example, we could go to sleep, sing, eat dinner, undress, dance, take out a flashlight and read the newspaper, carry on loud conversations, dribble a basketball up and down the aisles—these are just a handful of the millions of behaviors people are capable of. All of these possible paths vary in how much resistance we run into if we try to follow them. We discover this as soon as we choose paths we're not supposed to. Jump up and start singing, for example, and you'll quickly feel how much resistance the management and the rest of the audience offer up to discourage you from going any further. By comparison, the path of least resistance is far more appealing, which is why it's the one we're most likely to choose.

The odds are loaded toward a path of least resistance in several ways. We often choose a path because it's the only one we see. When I get on an elevator, for example, I turn and face front along with everyone else. It rarely occurs to me to do it another way, such as facing the rear. If I did, I'd soon feel how some paths have more resistance than others.

I once tested this idea by walking to the rear of an elevator and standing with my back toward the door. As the seconds ticked by, I could feel people looking at me, wondering what I was up to, and actually wanting me to turn around. I wasn't saying anything or doing anything to anyone. I was only standing there minding my own business. But that wasn't all that I was doing, for I was also violating a social norm that makes facing the door a path of least resistance. The path is there all the time—it's built in to riding the elevator as a social situation—but the path wasn't clear until I stepped onto a different one and felt the greater resistance rise up around it.

Similar dynamics operate around issues of difference and privilege. In many corporations, for example, the only way to get promoted is to have a mentor or sponsor pick you out as a promising person and bring you along by teaching you what you need to know and acting as an advocate who opens doors and creates opportunities. In a society that separates and privileges people by gender and race, there aren't many opportunities to get comfortable with people across lines of difference. This means that senior managers will feel drawn to employees who resemble them, which usually means those who are white, straight, and male.

Managers who are white and/or male probably won't realize they're following a path of least resistance that shapes their choice until they're asked to mentor an African American woman or someone else they don't resemble. The greater resistance toward the path of mentoring across difference may result from something as subtle as feeling "uncomfortable" in the other person's presence. But that's all it takes to make the relationship ineffective or to ensure that it never happens in the first place.[3] And as each manager follows the system's path to mentor and support those who most resemble them, the patterns of white dominance and male dominance in the system as a whole are perpetuated, regardless of what people consciously feel or intend.

In other cases, people know alternative paths exist, but they stick to the path of least resistance anyway, because they're afraid of what will happen if they don't. Resistance can take many forms, ranging from mild disapproval to being fired from a job, beaten up, run out of town, imprisoned, tortured, or killed. When managers are told to lay off large numbers of workers, for example, they may hate the assignment and feel a huge amount of distress. But the path of *least* resistance is to do what they're told, because the alternative may be for them to lose their own jobs. To make it less unpleasant, they may use euphemisms like "downsizing" and "outplacement" to soften the painful reality of people losing their jobs. (Note in this example how the path of least resistance isn't necessarily an easy path to follow.)

In similar ways, a man may feel uncomfortable when he hears a friend tell a sexist joke, and feel compelled to object in some way. But the path of least resistance in that situation is to go along and avoid the risk of being ostracized or ridiculed for challenging his friend and making *him* feel uncomfortable. The path of least resistance is to smile or laugh or just remain silent.

What we experience as social life happens through a complex dynamic between all kinds of systems—families, schools, workplaces, communities, entire societies—and the choices people make as they participate in them and help make them happen. How we experience the world and ourselves, our sense of other people, and the ongoing reality of the systems themselves all arise, take shape, and happen through this dynamic. In this way, social life produces a variety of consequences, including privilege and oppression. To understand that and what we can do to change it, we have to see how systems are organized in ways that encourage people to follow paths of least resistance. The existence of those paths and the choice we make to follow them are keys to what creates and perpetuates all the forms that privilege and oppression can take in people's lives.

WHAT IT MEANS TO BE INVOLVED IN PRIVILEGE AND OPPRESSION

Individuals and systems are connected to each other through a dynamic relationship. If we use this relationship as a model for thinking about the world and ourselves, it's easier to bring problems like racism, sexism, and heterosexism out into the open and talk about them. In particular, it's easier to see the problems in relation to us, and to see ourselves in relation to them.

If we think the world is just made up of individuals, then a white woman who's told she's "involved" in racism is going to think you're telling her she's a racist person who harbors ill will toward people of color. She's using an individualistic model of the world that limits her to interpreting words like *racist* as personal characteristics, personality flaws. Individualism divides the world up into different kinds of people—good people and bad, racists and nonracists, "good guys" and sexist pigs. It encourages us to think of racism, sexism, and heterosexism as diseases that infect people and make them sick. And so we look for a "cure" that will turn diseased, flawed individuals into healthy, "good" ones, or at least isolate them so that they can't infect others. And if we can't cure them, then we can at least try to control their behavior.

But what about everyone else? How do we see *them* in relation to the trouble around difference? What about the vast majority of whites, for example, who tell survey interviewers that they aren't racist and don't hate or even dislike people of color? Or what about the majority of men who say they favor an Equal Rights Amendment to the U.S. Constitution? From an individualistic perspective, if you aren't consciously or openly prejudiced or hurtful, then you aren't part of the problem. You might show disapproval of "bad" people and even try to help out the people who are hurt by them. Beyond that, however, the trouble doesn't have anything to do with you so far as you can see. If your feelings and thoughts and outward behavior are good, then *you* are good, and that's all that matters.

Unfortunately, that isn't all that matters. There's more, because patterns of oppression and privilege are rooted in systems that we all participate in and make happen. Those patterns are built into paths of least resistance that people feel drawn to follow every day, regardless of whether they think about where they lead or the consequences they produce. When male professors take more seriously students who look like themselves, for example, they don't have to be self-consciously sexist in order to help perpetuate patterns of gender privilege. They don't have to be bad people in order to play a "game" that produces oppressive consequences. It's the same as when people play Monopoly—it always ends with someone winning and everyone else losing, *because that's how the game is set up to work as a system.* The only way to change the outcome is to change how we see and play the game and, eventually, the *system itself* and its paths of least resistance. If we have a vision of what we want social life to look like, we have to create paths that lead in that direction.

Of course there are people in the world who have hatred in their hearts—such as neo-Nazi skinheads who make a sport of harassing and killing blacks or homosexuals—and it's important not to minimize the damage they do. Paradoxically, however, even though they cause a lot of trouble, they aren't the key to understanding privilege or to doing something about it. They are participating in something larger than themselves that, among other things, steers them toward certain targets for their rage. It's no accident that their hatred is rarely directed at privileged groups, but instead those who are culturally devalued and excluded. Hate-crime perpetrators may have personality disorders that bend them toward victimizing *someone,* but their choice of whom to victimize isn't part of a mental illness. That's something they have to learn, and culture is everyone's most powerful teacher. In choosing their targets, they follow paths of least resistance built into a society that everyone participates in, that everyone makes happen, regardless of how they feel or what they intend.

So if I notice that someone plays Monopoly in a ruthless way, it's a mistake to explain that simply in terms of their personality. I also have to ask how a system like Monopoly rewards ruthless behavior more than other games we might play. I have to ask how it creates conditions that make such behavior appear to be the path of least resistance, normal and unremarkable. And since I'm playing the game, too, I'm one of the people who make it happen as a system, and its paths must affect me, too.

My first reaction might be to deny that I follow that path. I'm not a ruthless person or anything close to it. But this misses the key difference between systems and the people who participate in them: We don't have to be ruthless *people* in order to support or follow paths of least resistance that lead to behavior with ruthless *consequences*. After all, we're all trying to win, because that's the point of the game. However gentle and kind I am as I take your money when you land on my Boardwalk with its four houses, take it I will and gladly, too. "Thank you," I say in my most sincerely unruthless tone, or even "Sorry," as I drive you out of the game by taking your last dollar and your mortgaged properties. Me, ruthless? Not at all. I'm just playing the game the way it's supposed to be played. And even if I don't try hard to win, the mere fact that I play the game supports its existence and makes it possible, especially if I remain silent about the consequences it produces. Just my going along makes the game appear normal and acceptable, which reinforces the paths of least resistance for everyone else.

This is how most systems work and how most people participate in them. It's also how systems of privilege work. Good people with good intentions make systems happen that produce all kinds of injustice and suffering for people in culturally devalued and excluded groups. Most of the time, people don't even know the paths are there in the first place, and this is why it's important to raise awareness that everyone is always following them in one way or another. If you weren't following a path of least resistance, you'd certainly know it, because you'd be on an alternative path with greater resistance that would make itself felt.

In other words, if you're not going along with the system, it won't be long before people notice and let you know it. All you have to do is show up for work wearing "inappropriate" clothes to see how quickly resistance can form around alternative paths.

The trouble around difference is so pervasive, so long-standing, so huge in its consequences for so many millions of people that it can't be written off as the misguided doings of a small minority of people with personality problems. The people who get labeled as bigots, misogynists, or homophobes are all following racist, sexist, heterosexist paths of least resistance that are built into the entire society.

In a way, "bad people" are like ruthless Monopoly players who are doing just what the game calls for even if their "style" is a bit extreme. Such extremists may be the ones who grab the headlines, but they don't have enough power to create and sustain trouble of this magnitude. The trouble appears in the daily workings of every workplace, every school and university, every government agency, every community. It involves every major kind of social system, and since systems don't exist without the involvement of people, there's no way to escape being involved in the trouble that comes out of them. If we participate in systems the trouble comes out of, and if those systems exist only through our participation, then this is enough to involve us in the trouble itself.

Reminders of this reality are everywhere. I see it, for example, every time I look at the label in a piece of clothing. I just went upstairs to my closet and noted where each of my shirts was made. Although each carries a U.S. brand name, only three were made here; the rest were made in the Philippines, Thailand, Mexico, Taiwan, Macao, Singapore, or Hong Kong. And although each cost me twenty to forty dollars, it's a good bet that the people who actually made them—primarily women— were paid pennies for their labor performed under terrible conditions that can sometimes be so extreme as to resemble slavery.

The only reason people exploit workers in such horrible ways is to make money in a capitalist system. To judge from the contents of my closet, that clearly includes *my* money. By itself, that fact doesn't make me a bad person, because I certainly don't intend that people suffer for the sake of my wardrobe. But it does mean that I'm involved in their suffering because I participate in a system that produces that suffering. As someone who helps make the system happen, however, I can also be a part of the solution.

But isn't the difference I could make a tiny one? The question makes me think of the devastating floods of 1993 along the Mississippi and Missouri rivers. The news was full of powerful images of people from all walks of life working feverishly side by side to build dikes to hold back the raging waters that threatened their communities. Together, they filled and placed thousands of sandbags. When the waters receded, much had been lost, but a great deal had been saved as well. I wonder how it felt to be one of those people. I imagine they were proud of their effort and experienced a satisfying sense of solidarity with the people they'd worked with. The sandbags each individual personally contributed were the tiniest fraction of the total, but each felt part of the group effort and was proud to identify with the consequences it produced. They didn't have to make a big or even measurable difference to feel involved.

It works that way with the good things that come out of people pulling together in all the systems that make up social life. It also works that way with the bad things, with each sandbag adding to the problem instead of the solution. To perpetuate privilege and oppression, we don't even have to do anything consciously to support it. Just our silence is crucial for ensuring its future, for the simple fact is that no system of social oppression can continue to exist without most people choosing to remain silent about it. If most whites spoke out about racism; if most men talked about sexism; if most heterosexuals came out of their closet of silence and stood openly against heterosexism, it would be a critical first step toward revolutionary change. But the vast majority of "good" people are silent on these issues, and it's easy for others to read their silence as support.

As long as we participate in social systems, we don't get to choose whether to be involved in the consequences they produce. We're involved simply through the fact that we're here. As such, we can only choose *how* to be involved, whether to be just part of the problem or also to be part of the solution. That's where our power lies, and also our responsibility.

CHAPTER 8

How Systems of Privilege Work

Like everything else in social life, privilege, power, and oppression exist only through social systems and how individuals participate in them. People make systems and their consequences happen; systems include paths of least resistance that shape who people are and how they participate. To see how all of that works, we need to look at how systems are put together. If we look at the game of Monopoly as a system, for example, we can describe it without ever talking about the personalities of the people who might play it. We can do the same thing with a university, a corporation, a family, a society, or a world economic system like global capitalism.

Systems organized around privilege have three key characteristics. They are *dominated* by privileged groups, *identified* with privileged groups, and *centered* on privileged groups. All three characteristics support the idea that members of privileged groups are superior to those below them and, therefore, deserve their privilege. A patriarchy, for example, is male-dominated, male-identified, and male-centered.[1] Race privilege happens through systems that are white-dominated, white-identified, and white-centered, and heterosexism works through systems that are dominated, identified with, and centered on heterosexuality and heterosexuals.

DOMINANCE

When we say that a system is dominated by a privileged group, it means that positions of power tend to be occupied by members of that group. Power also tends to be identified with such people in ways that make it seem normal and natural for them to have it. In a patriarchy, for example, power is culturally gendered in that it is associated primarily with men. To the people living in such a society, power looks "natural" on a man, but unusual and even problematic on a woman, marking her as an exception that calls for special scrutiny and some kind of explanation. When Margaret Thatcher was prime minister of Great Britain, for example, she was often referred to as "the Iron Lady." This drew attention to both her strength as a leader and the need to mark it as an exception. There would be no such need to mark a strong male prime minister (as an "Iron Man," for example), because his power would be assumed.

This kind of thinking supports a structure that allocates most power to men. In almost every organization, the farther down you look in the power structure, the more numerous women are; the higher up you go, the fewer women you'll find. That's what a male-dominated system looks like.

Just because a system is male-dominated doesn't mean that most men are powerful. As most men will tell you, they aren't, most often due to class or race. Male dominance does mean, however, that every man can *identify* with power as a value that his culture associates with manhood, which makes it easier for any man to assume and use power in relation to others. It also encourages a sense of entitlement in men to use women to meet their personal needs, whether it's getting coffee for everyone or taking the minutes of a meeting. Since women are culturally *dis*identified with power, it's harder for them to exercise it in any situation. When women do find ways to be powerful in relation to men, it's usually *in spite of* the male-dominated character of patriarchal systems as a whole.

For women to have power in relation to men also makes women vulnerable, because power in their hands lacks the cultural legitimacy of men's power. As such, it easily arouses suspicion. Female professors, for example, tell many stories of having their authority, expertise, and professional commitment routinely challenged not only by colleagues, but by students, men in particular.[2] As a man, I enjoy the benefit of the doubt with students, who usually assume I know what I'm talking about. When a woman walks into the same classroom, however, male students may challenge her credibility and authority from the start. They'll argue or question every point and feel free to interrupt her. They may go so far as to mutter "Bitch" to a pal in the next seat or comment on her physical appearance, or turn away, roll their eyes, go to sleep, hold side conversations.

"I'm still routinely asked if I've ever taught the course before," says one seasoned female professor. "They look utterly shocked when I say I've taught most of my courses 15–18 years—sometimes longer than they've been alive."[3]

Similar things can happen with peers. After teaching her first class, a new professor saw a male faculty member poke his head into her classroom after the students left. "Are you a faculty member here?" he asked.

"Yes," she said.

"Do you have a doctorate?"

"Yes."

"Well, at least you're educated," he said, and walked away.[4]

Powerful women are also open to being called bitches or lesbians as a way to discredit and negate their power by attacking them personally. When women gather together, even just for lunch, men may suspect them of "being up to something"—planning some subversive use of power that needs to be monitored and contained. Men's anxiety over this usually comes out as humor ("So, what little plot are you gals hatching?") but the gender dynamic underlying male dominance and women's potential to subvert it is clearly there. In the home—the one place where women manage to carve out some power for themselves—their power is routinely seen as problematic in ways that men's power in relation to women is not. The abundance of insulting terms for men who are dominated by women, for example, and the absence of such insults for comparable women show clearly how our culture sanctions male dominance.

That patriarchy is male-dominated also doesn't mean that most men have domineering personalities that make them need or want to control others. In other words, I'm not using the term *male dominance* to describe men. Rather, it describes a patriarchal system that both men and women participate in. It also describes gendered patterns of unequal power and paths of least resistance for both men and women that support those patterns.

For men, those paths of least resistance include presenting the appearance of being in control of themselves, others, and events. I'm aware of this path, for example, in how I feel drawn to respond to questions whether I know the answer or not, to interrupt in conversations, to avoid admitting that I'm wrong about anything, and to take up room in public spaces. One day some years ago, my life partner Nora Jamieson and I were having a conversation about something that began when she raised a question. I responded almost without hesitation, until she interrupted me to ask, "Do you actually know that or are you just saying it?" I was startled to realize that I was just saying it. The response appeared in my head and that seemed reason enough to say it. But I wasn't saying it as though it was just a thought that happened to be wandering through my mind. I spoke with an unhesitating flow that suggested I knew what I was talking about, that I was an expert in the subject she'd raised.

But I didn't know that what I was saying was true, at least no more true than what anyone else might say, provided, of course, that I gave them the chance. This included Nora, who had been sitting there listening to me in silence. Until that moment, she followed a corresponding path of least resistance for women: silent attentiveness, hesitation, self-doubt, humility, deference, supporting what men say and do, and taking up as little space as possible. When she stepped off that path, she shook an entire structure by revealing its existence and how both of us were participating in it. She also raised the possibility of alternative paths—of men learning about silence and listening, doubt and uncertainty, supporting others and sharing space.

Why call such patterns of control and deference "paths of least resistance"? Why not just say that I and many other men have a problem we might call a "controlling personality" or that women just tend to be "unassertive"? The answer is that we all swim in a dominant culture that is full of images of men seeking control, taking up time and space, competing with other men, and living with a sense of entitlement in relation to women. And each of those is matched by images of women letting men do all of that, if not encouraging them to or insisting on it. The images permeate popular culture—from film and television to advertising and literature—and shape the news, from the front page to the sports section.

What these images do is place a value on male power and control that is used every day as a standard for evaluating men in almost every aspect of their lives. Men who live up to it are routinely rewarded with approval, while men who seem insufficiently decisive and manly are always vulnerable to ridicule and scorn, primarily from other men. And so if I feel drawn to control a conversation or to always have an answer, it isn't simply because I'm a controlling *person,* no more than greedy behavior happens in a Monopoly game just because people are greedy.

This is what Deborah Tannen misses in her popular books on gender and talk.[5] She describes many gender differences in styles of talking that tend to give men control over conversations. But when she tries to explain why this is so, she almost completely ignores how those differences promote male privilege at women's expense. Instead she argues that women and men talk differently because as children they played in same-sex groups and learned distinctively male or female ways of speaking from their peers. What she doesn't tell us is how those peers happened to acquire their gendered styles of talking. The answer is that they learned them from adults in families, the mass media, and in school. In other words, they learned them by participating in a society where conversation is a major arena in which gender privilege is played out.

Patterns of dominance and the paths of least resistance that sustain them show up in every system of privilege. White dominance, for example, is reflected in an unequal racial balance of power in society and its institutions. The same is true of heterosexuality, although so many lesbians and gay men are still in the closet that it's hard to be sure about the sexual orientation of people in power. There is no ambiguity or lack of clarity in the mainstream culture, however. It's rare to see a film or television show in which the most powerful character is identified as gay, lesbian, working class, or African American, Latino/a, or Asian, or if they are, to have them still be alive when the closing credits begin to roll. Working-class characters are rarely the focus in films and on television, and when they do appear they are routinely portrayed as criminals or as stupid, ignorant, crude, bigoted, shallow, and immoral.[6] The closest that racial minorities get to powerful roles is as sidekicks to powerful whites in "buddy" movies, and exceptions like *The Color Purple* and *The*

Hurricane are few and far between and must struggle for whatever recognition they get. And in a heterosexist culture, a powerful gay man is a contradiction in terms, and powerful lesbians are often dismissed as not being real women at all.

The result of such patterns of dominance is that if you're female, gay, African American, Latino/a, Asian, Native American, or in some other way on the outside of privilege, when you look upward in all kinds of power structures you don't see people like you. Your interests are not represented where power is wielded and rewards are distributed, and you get no encouragement to imagine yourself as one of those who enjoy power and rewards. Those who don't look like people in power will feel invisible and in fact *be* invisible, for they are routinely overlooked. And this is a major way that patterns of inequality and privilege repeat themselves over and over again.

IDENTIFIED WITH PRIVILEGE

"It's a man's world" is an expression that points in part to the male-dominated character of society which puts most power in the hands of men. In the same way, one could say "It's a white world" or "It's a straight world." But there's more than power at work here, for privileged groups are also usually taken as the standard of comparison that represents the best that society has to offer. This is what it means to say that a system is male-identified or white-identified.

On most college campuses, for example, black students feel pressured to talk, dress, and act like middle-class whites in order to fit in and be accepted, what some have called being "Afro-Saxon."[7] In similar ways, most workplaces define appropriate appearance and ways of speaking in terms that are culturally associated with being white, from clothing and hairstyles to diction and slang. Racial and ethnic minorities experience being marked as outsiders, to the extent that many navigate the social world by consciously changing how they talk from one situation to another. In shopping for an apartment over the telephone, for example, many African Americans know they have to "talk white" in order to be accepted (which may come to nothing once they show up in person and discover that the apartment has "just" been rented).[8]

Because privileged groups are assumed to represent society as a whole, "American," for example, is culturally defined as white, in spite of the diversity of the population. You can see this in a statement like, "Americans must learn to be more tolerant of other races." I doubt that most people would see this as saying that we need Asians to be more tolerant of whites or blacks to be more tolerant of Native Americans. The "Americans" are assumed to be white, and the "other races" are assumed to be races *other* than white. *Other* is the key word in understanding how systems are identified with privileged groups. The privileged group is the assumed "we" in relation to "them." The "other" is the "you people" whom the "we" regard as problematic, unacceptable, unlikable, or beneath "our" standards.

In a white-identified system, white is the assumed race unless something other than white is marked—hence the common use of the term *nonwhite* to lump together a variety of races into a single category of "other" in relation to a white standard. To get a sense of the effect of this practice, imagine a society in which whites were referred to routinely as "noncoloreds."

White identification means that whether arrested for a crime or winning a Nobel prize, whites are rarely if ever identified *as* white, because that is assumed. Racial tags are common, however, for everyone else, from "black physician" and "African American writer" to "Asian actor." If a small group of white citizens marched on Washington to protest a policy that had nothing to do with race, news reports wouldn't mention their race and certainly wouldn't try to figure out why the group was all-white. They would simply be described as protesters or citizens or members of a group that takes a position on that policy. If a group of Mexican Americans did the same thing, they would surely be identified as such and be asked why there weren't any whites among them. And this isn't because Mexican Americans stand out as a numerical minority, since the same pattern would hold for women, who would "stand out" and be tagged as women even though they outnumber men in the population.

Such patterns of identification are especially powerful in relation to gender. It is still common to use masculine pronouns to refer to people in general or to use *man* to name the entire species (as in "mankind" and "the family of man"). In a similar way, men and manhood are held up as standards of comparison. The idea of "brotherhood," for example, is clearly gendered, since women can't be brothers by any stretch of the imagination, yet it also carries powerful cultural meaning about *human* connection, as in the stirring line from "America the Beautiful," "And crown thy good with brotherhood from sea to shining sea."[9] Brotherhood is defined as a "condition" or "quality" of human relationship (see Box 8.1) that embodies warmth and good feeling, especially across social differences. It is linked to the idea of *fellowship*—the general human capacity for companionship, common interest or feeling, friendliness, and communion—which is based on being a fellow, which is also clearly and unambiguously defined as male. By comparison, although African American women have made powerful use of the idea of sisterhood, in the dominant patriarchal culture it amounts to little more than the biological fact of being someone's sister, which is to say, being female and sharing the same set of parents. All of its other meanings are narrowly confined to groups of women—such as nuns and feminists—even when it refers to the quality of relationships.

In short, men are the cultural standard for humanity; women are just women. So when a woman is celebrated at the office and everyone joins in a round of "For She's a Jolly Good

---

Box 8.1
The Word "Brotherhood" as
an Instance of Male-Identified Language

Sisterhood
1. The state of being a sister.
2. A group of sisters, especially of nuns or of female members of a church.
3. An organization of women with a common interest.
4. Congenial relationship or companionship among women.
5. Community or network of women who participate in support of feminism.

Brotherhood
1. The condition or quality of being a brother.
2. The quality of being brotherly, **fellow**ship.
3. A fraternal or trade organization.
4. All those engaged in a particular trade or profession or sharing a common interest or quality.
5. The belief that all people should act with warmth and equality toward one another regardless of differences in race, creed, nationality, etc.

Fellow   A man or boy.

Fellowship
1. The condition or relation of being a fellow; the fellowship of humankind.
2. Friendly relationship.

Fellow," no one laughs at or objects to the oxymoron, because in a male-identified society, it's an honor to be considered "one of the guys," to be associated with men and the standards by which men are measured. Nor are many people disturbed by the fact that there are *no* words that culturally associate women with a valued quality of human relation in the way that *fellow* and *fellowship* do for men. If someone suggested changing the words of *America the Beautiful* to "and crown thy good with sisterhood," however, imagine the reception that idea would get and you have some idea of the power of male identification.

Male identification is woven into every aspect of social life. Most high-status occupations, for example, are organized around qualities that are culturally associated with masculinity, such as aggression, competitiveness, emotional detachment, and control. This is what it takes to succeed in law, medicine, science, academia, politics, sports, or business. No woman (or man) becomes a corporate manager, gets tenure at a university, or is elected to public office by showing their capacity for cooperation, sharing, emotional sensitivity, and nurturing.

This means that a man can make it as a lawyer or a manager while at the same time living up to the cultural standards that define a "real man." A woman, however, is caught in a bind. If she patterns herself on ideals that are culturally defined as feminine, she's likely to be seen as not having what it takes to get ahead in a male-identified world. But if she pursues a more "masculine" path toward success, she opens herself to being judged as not feminine enough—uncaring, cold, a bitch. Students hold their female college professors, for example, to a much higher standard of caring and emotional availability than they do male teachers. But if a woman professional comes across as *too* warm and caring, her credibility, competence, and authority are invariably undermined and challenged. In a male-identified system, she can't fit the model of a successful professional or manager and at the same time measure up as a "real woman." It is the kind of classic double bind that is one of the hallmarks of social oppression: She can be devalued no matter what she does.[10]

The world of work is also male-identified in the definition of a "career" and the timing of key stages in the route to success. In most organizations, for example, the idea of a career assumes an almost complete commitment to the work, which means that the only way to have both a career and a family is to have someone at home to take care of children and other domestic responsibilities. Despite all the talk about "the new fatherhood," this almost always means a wife and mother. Furthermore, in typical patterns of career timing, the key years for establishing yourself overlap with a woman's key years for starting a family. In this way, "serious" work is structured to fit most men's lives far more easily and with far less conflict than it fits most women's lives.[11] So *profession* and *career* are words that on the surface don't appear to be gendered one way or the other, but in fact they are implicitly male-identified.

Male identification shows up in more subtle ways as well, from popular culture to the comings and goings of everyday life. In Ken Burns's PBS documentary on baseball, for example, he tells us: "Baseball defines who we are." Apparently, he didn't give much thought to who is included in *we*. I doubt he meant that the essence of baseball defines who women are in some fundamental way or that it defines what most women experience as their society. But if the statement is likely to ring true for men, then, in a male-identified world, it's assumed that it rings true for everyone, and if it doesn't, so what?

In this way, male identification tends to make women invisible, just as white and heterosexual identification tend to make people of color, lesbians, and gay men invisible. The other day I made an airline reservation and the clerk gave me a confirmation code. "PWCEO," she said, and then, to make sure I'd gotten it right, added, "That's Peter, William, Charles, Edward, Oscar."

PRIVILEGE AT THE CENTER

Because systems are identified with privileged groups, the path of least resistance is to focus attention on them—who they are, what they do and say, and how they do it. Look at the front page of any newspaper, and you'll find that the vast majority of people pictured, quoted, and discussed are men who also happen to be white and middle or upper class. If women, Latinos, or African Americans are there, it's usually because of something that's been done to them (murdered, for example) or something they've done wrong (rioted, murdered, stole, cheated, and so on). There are exceptions, of course—a Madeleine Albright as Secretary of State or a Clarence Thomas as an associate justice of the Supreme Court or black athletes—one of the few areas where they are allowed to excel. As exceptions, however, they prove the rule.

To judge from television and film, most of what happens of significance in the world happens to straight white men. To see what I mean, try an experiment: Make a list of the ten most important movies ever made, movies that reflect something powerful and enduring about the human experience, about courage and personal transformation, the journey of the soul, the testing of character, finding out who we really are and what life is all about. Once you have your list, identify the key character in each, the one whose courage, transformation, journey, testing, and revelations are the point of the story. And then note that person's gender and race. Chances are that at least nine out of ten will be white, Anglo, heterosexual males, even though they are less than 20 percent of the U.S. population.

Consider, for example, the list of films that have been awarded the Oscar for best picture over the last thirty years (see Box 8.2). Of these films, judged better than all the rest in each year, none set in the United States places people of color at the center of the story without their having to share it with white characters of equal importance (*Driving Miss Daisy* and *In the Heat of the Night*). The one film that focuses on Native Americans (*Dances with Wolves*) is told from a white man's point of view with Native Americans clearly identified as the other. Only two focus on non-European cultures (*The Last Emperor* and *Gandhi*). Although *Out of Africa* is set in Africa, the story focuses exclusively on whites and, without any critical comment, their exploitation

---

Box 8.2
Academy Award Winning Films in the
Category "Best Picture," 1965–1999

1999	*American Beauty*	1981	*Chariots of Fire*
1998	*Shakespeare in Love*	1980	*Ordinary People*
1997	*Titanic*	1979	*Kramer vs. Kramer*
1996	*The English Patient*	1978	*The Deer Hunter*
1995	*Braveheart*	1977	*Annie Hall*
1994	*Forrest Gump*	1976	*Rocky*
1993	*Schindler's List*	1975	*One Flew Over the*
1992	*Unforgiven*		*Cuckoo's Nest*
1991	*The Silence of the Lambs*	1974	*The Godfather, Part II*
1990	*Dances with Wolves*	1973	*The Sting*
1989	*Driving Miss Daisy*	1972	*The Godfather, Part I*
1988	*Rain Man*	1971	*The French Connection*
1987	*The Last Emperor*	1970	*Patton*
1986	*Platoon*	1969	*Midnight Cowboy*
1985	*Out of Africa*	1968	*Oliver!*
1984	*Amadeus*	1967	*In the Heat of the Night*
1983	*Terms of Endearment*	1966	*A Man for All Seasons*
1982	*Gandhi*	1965	*The Sound of Music*

---

of the African continent. This same list of films also contains only three that are female-centered (*Out of Africa, Terms of Endearment,* and *The Sound of Music*), and none with any major characters who are gay or lesbian.

When a film does focus on someone who is other than white or male or heterosexual, it gets little attention unless, like *The Color Purple* (1985), it has a powerful white heterosexual male such as Steven Spielberg behind it. Anything less than that—no matter how good it is—has little chance of drawing much attention, much less winning an Academy Award. Even *The Color Purple,* which was nominated for eleven Academy Awards, didn't win a single one.

The handful of films that do focus on women or blacks or lesbians or gay men are likely to be tagged (and devalued) as "women's films" or "black films" or "gay films" or "lesbian films," even though all the rest are never called "men's films" or "white films" or "heterosexual films." In a society identified with males, whites, and heterosexuals, such films are supposedly about everyone, or at least everyone who counts.

Because systems of privilege center on dominant groups, those who aren't included have reason to feel invisible, because in an important social sense, they are. Black, Latino/a, and female students routinely report that instructors don't call on them in class, don't listen to what they say, or don't let them finish without interruption. Research shows that men receive the overwhelming majority of attention in classrooms at every level of education,[12] a pattern that repeats itself in the workplace and everywhere else that women and men meet. I've been in meetings of thirty people in which the two or three men present talked almost the entire time with no sign from anyone that anything was wrong.

This happens in part because in a world that centers attention on men and what they do and say, the path of least resistance for men is to claim attention by calling out answers without being recognized or by interrupting female students. It also happens because the path of least resistance for women is to give way in the face of privilege, to allow men to take up whatever time and space they want and not challenge their right to do so. So when male students jump in with a response—even to the extent of thinking up answers as they go along—teachers and female students let them get away with it.

When men don't jump in, teachers gravitate toward them anyway, standing closer to them in the room, looking to them for the most interesting or productive answers, challenging and coaching them more, all the while assuming that women don't have what it takes to say something worth hearing.[13] None of this has to be done consciously in order to center attention on dominant groups at the expense of everyone else. It simply flows along down a well-traveled path of least resistance that makes invisibility a key part of the devaluing that lies at the heart of privilege and oppression.

Often the only way that marginalized groups can get attention is to make an issue of how social life is centered on dominant groups. So women form their own support groups at work; they attend women's colleges, where they don't have to overcome the cultural weight of male-centeredness; blacks form their own dorms or clubs on college campuses and sit at their own tables in the dining hall;[14] schools create special programs that focus on women or African Americans or various ethnic groups; women participate in a "Take Our Daughters to Work" day; lesbians and gay men organize pride marches to draw attention to the simple fact that they exist ("We are everywhere").

Drawing attention away from dominant groups often provokes a defensive response that reaffirms the very privilege the trouble is about. In systems of privilege, the focus is on dominant groups all the time as a matter of course, so much that it's never recognized as something special. Thus the slightest deviation can be perceived as a profound loss of privilege. Some fascinating research on gender in the classroom, for example, shows that as long as men overwhelmingly dominate the conversation, the participation of women and men is perceived as *roughly equal.* But if women's talk rises to as little as a quarter or a third of the total interaction, men perceive that the women have taken over. Such perceived shifts can result in howls of protest over the unfairness of giving subordinate groups "special" attention—"Why not a 'Take Our Sons to Work Day'?" "Why do gays and lesbians have to call attention to themselves?" "When do we get to have a White History Month?"

As so often happens, subordinate groups are in a double bind. If they don't call attention to themselves, the defaults built into systems of privilege make them invisible and devalued. If they do call attention to themselves, if they dare to put themselves at the center, they risk being accused of being pushy or seeking special treatment. This is why women, gay men, lesbians, and racial or ethnic minorities are often referred to as "special-interest groups" that are always working from a biased agenda, while men, heterosexuals, and whites are not.

THE ISMS

Most of the time, words like *racism, sexism,* and *heterosexism* are used to describe how people feel and behave. Racism, for example, is seen as something that exists only inside people as a flawed part of their personalities. It's an attitude, a collection of stereotypes, a bad intention, a desire or need to discriminate or do harm, a form of hatred. From that perspective, doing something about racism means changing how individuals feel, think, and behave (since behavior is connected to how we think and feel).

But racism is also built in to the systems that people live and work in. It's embedded in a capitalist system organized around competition over scarce resources, and organized to be white-dominated, white-identified, and white-centered. This manifests itself everywhere we turn. Given this reality, it doesn't make sense to ignore everything but individual personality and behavior, as if we live in a social vacuum. For this reason, sociologist David Wellman argues for a broader definition of racism that includes but goes beyond the personal. Racism is the patterns of privilege and oppression themselves and *any*thing—intentional or not—that helps to create or perpetuate those patterns. If we extend this to other forms of privilege, then sexism and heterosexism are also more than personal expressions of hostility or prejudice, but include everything that people do or don't do that promotes male privilege and heterosexual privilege.[15]

To see what Wellman means, consider not what people do or say, but what they don't. Consider, for example, the power of silence to promote privilege and oppression. Human beings are highly dependent on one another for standards of what—and who—is okay and who isn't. Although there will always be individuals who don't care what other people think, the vast majority will avoid doing something they believe people around them would criticize. But if the people in their community and society are silent, then the perpetrators are free to interpret that as support for what they do.

From the late 1800s through the mid-1940s, for example, white Southerners lynched more than five thousand African Americans. The actual violence was done by a relatively small number of individuals, but they acted from the assumption that most people in their communities and states either approved of their actions or wouldn't do anything to stop them even if they disapproved. Many lynchings were advertised in advance in local newspapers, for example, and pictures taken of the atrocities were often sold as postcards.

Since the lynchers couldn't possibly know everyone in their community or state personally, the only way they could assume they'd get away with it was to see themselves as living in a particular kind of society—white-dominated, white-identified, and white-centered—that placed such a low value on black people's lives that torturing and killing them was unlikely to be made an issue, much less treated as a crime. The real power lay not with the lynchers as individuals, but with society and the great collective silence in the face of the racist horror the individuals perpetrated, a silence that spoke as loudly as the violence itself, regardless of how people felt about it as individuals.

Just as most Southerners (and Northerners) were silent about lynching, the vast majority of men are silent on the issue of sexual harassment and violence and do nothing more than privately disapprove of it or assure themselves that they'd never engage in it themselves. In the same way, most whites do nothing that would raise consciousness about all the ways racism works in their communities or workplaces. They may readily acknowledge overt behavior that perpetuates the trouble around difference. "Yes," they'll say when asked about discrimination, "it's a terrible thing." And they mean it.

What they don't see most of the time, however, is how silence and not looking and not asking are *in effect* just as racist or sexist or heterosexist *because oppression depends on them in order to continue.* White professors or managers who don't go out of their way to ask about race trouble in classrooms or the workplace may be good people who'd never act from ill will toward racial minorities. But how good or bad they are as people is beside the point. Their motives and intentions are irrelevant to the future of racism as a pattern of inequality and the suffering it causes. What counts isn't just what they do, but even more what they *don't* do.[16]

When I think about this, I imagine a scene in which a gang of white men are beating a black man in broad daylight on a city street. I'm standing in a crowd of white people who are watching. We aren't hurting anyone; we feel no ill will toward the man being beaten; we may be feeling sorry for him. We aren't cheering the attackers on or showing any outward signs of approval. We're just standing in silence, "minding our own business." And then one of the men stops, looks up, and says, his eyes panning across our faces, "We appreciate your support. We couldn't do it without you."

This is how racism and other forms of privilege really work day in and day out, as a result of what might be called "passive oppression." It depends on a social environment that makes it easy for so many to stand by and do nothing. Most white people in the United States are racist not because they act from feelings or thoughts of racial hostility or ill will, but simply "because they acquiesce in the large cultural order which continues the work of racism."[17] That's all that's required of most white people in order for racism to continue: that they not notice, that they do nothing, that they remain silent.

THE ISMS AND US

It is tempting for whites, for men, and for heterosexuals to suppose that they could be raised in a racist, sexist, and heterosexist society and participate in it day after day without being touched by it on a personal level. But it's a dream that, for everyone else, is a nightmare of denial. There is no way for a member of a dominant group to escape that kind of immersion unscathed. Nobody is the exception who miraculously doesn't internalize any of the negative ideas, attitudes, or images that pour in a steady stream from the surrounding culture and make the trouble around privilege happen as it does.

In other words, on some level, *of course* I'm racist, sexist, and heterosexist in the same way that I automatically dream in English and prefer certain foods. I wish it weren't so, but it is. The assumption that some racism resides in every white person is a reasonable one in this society.[18] I would assume that everyone I meet in the United States speaks English until they showed otherwise, not because of what I know about them, but because of what I know about the culture of this society. In the same way, I would assume that racism touches and shapes everyone in one way or another and leaves a mark that cannot be erased. To assume otherwise is to engage in wishful thinking and live in a world that doesn't exist.

This doesn't mean that white people are consciously racist or that men are intentionally sexist, or that heterosexuals are overtly heterosexist. But it does mean that there isn't a single white person or man or heterosexual who doesn't have these issues to deal with inside and in relation to the world around them. This is their legacy. It was handed to them when they were children with no sense of what was wise and good to take into themselves and what was not. And so they accepted it, uncritically, unknowingly, even innocently, but accept it they did. It wasn't their fault. They have no reason to feel guilty about it, because they didn't *do* anything. But now it is there for them to deal with, just as it's there for women, people of color, lesbians, and gay men who *also* didn't do anything to deserve the oppression that so profoundly shapes their lives.

CHAPTER 9

Getting Off the Hook
Denial and Resistance

No one likes to see themselves as connected to someone else's misery, no matter how remote the link. Usually their first response is to find a way to get themselves off the hook, and as I'll show below, there are all kinds of ways to do that. As a result, they leave it to someone else to take care of the problem, which, of course, doesn't happen, and for pretty much the same reasons.

The fact is that we're all on the hook because there's no way to avoid being part of the problem. People of color, the lower and working classes, women gay and straight, and gay men are all on the hook every day. Whites, heterosexuals, and men are, too, but they're more likely not to know it because they have so many ways to act as though they aren't, and privilege allows them to get away with it. But, the more aware we are of all the ways there are to fool ourselves, the easier it is to become part of the solution.[1]

DENY AND MINIMIZE

Perhaps the easiest way to get off the hook is to deny the hook exists in the first place.

"Racism and sexism used to be problems, but they aren't anymore."

"The American Dream is alive and well and available to everyone."

"There are no gays or lesbians where I work, so sexual orientation isn't an issue here."

"Affirmative action has actually turned the tables—if anyone's in trouble now, it's whites and men." Or, as a recent cover of the *Atlantic Monthly* magazine proclaimed, "Girls Rule!"[2]

Closely related to denial is minimizing the trouble by acknowledging that it exists but doesn't amount to much. When women and people of color are accused of "whining," for example, they're essentially being told that whatever they have to deal with isn't that bad and they should "just get on with it." When you deny the reality of oppression, you also deny the reality of the privilege that underlies it, which is just what it takes to get off the hook.

When whites, straights, or men practice this kind of denial, it rarely seems to occur to them that they're in a poor position to know what they're talking about. For them to act as though they know better than others what they are up against is just the sort of presumption that privilege encourages. Privilege invites them to define other people's experience for them, to tell them what it's like to be them regardless of what they say it's like. Adults do this all the time with children. A child falls down and cries and an adult might say, "Now, now, stop crying; it doesn't hurt that much," when in fact the adult has no way of knowing how much it hurts. Or the child wakes up with a nightmare and adults might tell them, "There's nothing to be afraid of," when that may not be true at all for the child. In similar ways, all members of various privileged groups are culturally authorized to interpret other people's experience for them, to deny the validity of their own reports, and to impose their views of reality.

Denial also takes the form of seeing subordinate groups as actually being *better off* than privileged groups. An acquaintance of mine, for example, often remarks with a sense of envy on the qualities black people have had to develop to survive in the face of centuries of racism. She sees in them a strength and depth of soul and feeling that she'd like to have herself. Whenever the subject of racism comes up, her first response is to counter with a list of black "advantages," as if weighing them in the balance against her privileged position as a white woman. Her tone is a mixture of longing and resentment, as if she feels put upon to have to consider white privilege for even a moment when she feels such a lack in her own life. The paradoxical idea that envy and privilege can and often do exist side by side doesn't occur to her as she defends herself against seeing what she'd rather not see.

BLAME THE VICTIM

One can acknowledge that privilege and oppression exist and even that they have terrible consequences for people and still get off the hook by blaming it all on them.[3] Whites can draw on a rich supply of negative cultural stereotypes, for example, to satisfy themselves that if people of color were different—if they were more like whites supposedly are—there wouldn't be so much trouble. Whites can say things like, "If blacks were smarter or worked harder or got an education, they'd be okay," and expect most other whites to go along, because racist stereotypes have such authority in this culture. They can also count on whites who disagree with them not to say so to their face.

In similar ways, men can tell themselves that women who say they're sexually harassed are hypersensitive, or had no business being where they were, or sent mixed signals, or "asked for it" in one way or another. If a woman fails to break through the glass ceiling, men can say she doesn't have the right stuff. If she allows herself to be openly emotional, men can point to that as a reason she hasn't reached the heights; if she *isn't* emotional and nurturing, they can criticize her for not being "womanly" enough, too much like a man. If she's friendly, men can say she wants to be approached sexually; if she isn't friendly, they can say she's stuck up, cold, a bitch even, and deserves what she gets.

Or lesbians and gay men may be told they're "asking for trouble" by "flaunting" their sexual orientation by, say, holding hands in public—in other words, by being as open about being gay or lesbian as heterosexuals are about being straight.

The result of such thinking is that oppression is blamed on the people who suffer most from it, while privilege and those who benefit remain invisible and relatively untouched. And off the hook.

CALL IT SOMETHING ELSE

A more subtle way to deny oppression and privilege is to call them something else, thereby creating the appearance of being in touch with reality without having to do something about it.

Gender inequality, for example, is often described as a charming "battle of the sexes," or as an anthropological curiosity based on the idea that males and females come from different cultures, if not different planets. Deborah Tannen tells us in her popular books on gender and language that the problem is primarily one of communication and misunderstanding. The two genders come from essentially different cultures, she writes, and they get into trouble because they don't know how to interpret each other's talk. In fact, however, they grow up in the same culture. They live in the same families, attend the same schools, watch television and movies together, and play in the same neighborhoods and schoolyards.

And while gender differences in styles of talk do exist, they are more significant than the differences between, say, Japanese and U.S. styles of talk. The differences serve a purpose. They ensure male privilege and keep women in an inferior position. They reflect the male-dominated, male-centered, male-identified nature of society. Every time a man interrupts a woman, for example, and she defers by becoming silent, a pattern of male dominance and male centeredness is acted out once again, one of the endless tiny events through which social systems and gender privilege happen. There's nothing cute or charming about it, but acting as if there were is a way to avoid looking at what's really going on.

Avoiding the trouble by calling it something else is most highly developed in relation to gender inequality. A major reason is that women and men depend on one another in ways that other groups do not. Most whites don't particularly need people of color, for example, but relationships across gender lines are the backbone of most people's lives. This is especially true for heterosexuals, but no matter what your sexual orientation, everyone has parents and most have siblings or friendships that are cross-gender. So how do we live in such close quarters without confronting the reality—and the discomfort—of the trouble around gender? Patriarchal culture provides the answer: to see the world through a thick ideology of gender, a rich collection of images and ideas that mask the reality of gender inequality by turning it into something else in our minds.

Men find ways to make jokes, for example, about every aspect of gender inequality, from violence against women to sexuality to who gets stuck with cleaning the house or changing the diapers. They laugh about it in ways that would be unthinkable if the subject were race or anti-Semitism. This isn't because gender oppression is less serious than other forms. In many ways just the opposite is true. Instead, it is because gender inequality runs so deep in our lives and has such serious consequences that men go to even greater lengths to make it appear normal and so avoid seeing it for what it is.

IT'S BETTER THIS WAY

The combination of denial and calling oppression and privilege something else often results in the claim that everyone actually prefers things the way they are. I often hear whites, for example, say with great confidence that blacks would rather live among other blacks, reflecting a supposedly natural human tendency to choose the company of "your own kind." In fact, however, research shows clearly that most blacks would prefer to live in integrated neighborhoods. If anyone wants to live "with their own kind," it is whites. It is whites who enforce the extreme level of residential segregation found in the United States and the devastating consequences that result.

Segregation is also portrayed as a matter of simple economics: blacks and other people of color don't live among whites because they can't afford to. But in fact, it is racism, not income, occupation, or education, that stands in the way of integrated living for most people of color, especially those in the middle class.[4]

The thick ideology around gender privilege includes all kinds of claims that the status quo is best. Patriarchal culture, for example, is full of messages that women prefer strong men who dominate them and make all the "big" decisions: When a woman says no to sex, she at least means maybe and probably means yes; women "ask" for all kinds of trouble, especially what's otherwise known as rape, sexual harassment, and being beaten by domestic partners; male superiority is a natural arrangement dictated by genes and other biological imperatives; men are naturally breadwinners, and women are naturally best suited to having bread won for them and tending to children and keeping the house clean. It doesn't matter how much evidence is weighed against such notions. It doesn't matter how often women complain about male control or how often they insist that no means no. It doesn't matter that women have been major "breadwinners" for virtually all of human history and that staying home and being supported by men is a historical anomaly that doesn't apply to the vast majority of people in the world and never has.

The truth doesn't matter, however, because ideology isn't about truth or accuracy. Rather, its purpose is to get privileged people off the hook and preserve the status quo. It supports the all too human tendency to soothe yourself into thinking there's nothing unpleasant or challenging here to deal with, and certainly nothing to do with you. And when someone dares to challenge that comforting reality, it's easy to confuse the bearer of bad news with the bad news itself. When blacks call attention to the divisions caused by race privilege, for example, they're often accused of *creating* those divisions, as if racism isn't a problem unless you talk about it. Talking about privilege rather than privilege itself gets defined as the problem.

Being part of the solution to a trouble that already divides us begins with coming together around the simple truth that we're *all* in trouble and that pretending we aren't is a key to what keeps us apart.

IT DOESN'T COUNT
IF YOU DON'T MEAN IT

Because our culture encourages us to use an individual-guilt model to explain just about everything that goes wrong, it's easy to confuse intentions with consequences. In other words, if something bad happens, someone's conscious bad intentions must be behind it. A corollary is that if your intentions are good, then nothing bad can happen from them.

As we saw earlier, for example, racism is usually defined as a bad attitude toward people of color, as malicious intentions buttressed by negative cultural stereotypes. When whites are confronted with matters of race, they usually react as if the issue isn't patterns of inequality and unnecessary suffering, but their own personal feelings and views about race and the question of their individual guilt or innocence. They respond as if the challenge is to get themselves off the hook by showing themselves to be pure on the subject of race. They seem to think that if they don't *mean* it, then it didn't happen, as if their conscious intent is the only thing that connects them to the consequences of what they do or don't do.

"I didn't mean it" stops conversation before people can get to the reality that it doesn't matter whether they meant it or not. The consequence remains just the same. Take the case of a white female professor who calls on only whites in class. Since she has no conscious animosity toward people of color, she doesn't see herself as having anything to do with the continuing pattern of racial inequality that results from the choices she makes as she does her job. In other words, she doesn't see herself as part of the problem or, therefore, as part of the solution.

Or a man makes repeated sexual comments to a female colleague. When she gets angry and tells him to stop, he gets defensive. He says it was only a joke, or that he just finds her attractive and meant no harm by it. What he doesn't do is acknowledge that regardless of the intentions he's aware of, he *has* done her harm, and she's likely to be left to deal with it on her own. He acts as though a lack of conscious intent means a lack of effect, as if *saying* it was only a joke or only being *aware* of it as a joke is enough to *make* it just a joke.

Sometimes this insight can take us into unexpected places when we apply it to the mundane details of everyday life. A while ago, for example, there was a heated exchange in an Internet discussion over what seems at first glance to be a trivial topic: whether men should open doors for women. A middle-aged man at a talk I gave recently expressed his frustration and concern about whether to open doors for women. "The rules are changing," he said. "I always thought it was the polite thing to do, but now women get mad at me sometimes."

The online discussion began when a woman pointed out that she didn't like it when men rushed ahead or, worse, jockeyed with other men for the honor of opening a door for her to pass through without having to open it herself.

"I remember," she wrote, "when I first realized how stupid I felt sitting in a car while a man scurried around to open the door for me." She objected to this "door-opening ceremony" because "it seemed to do more for men than it did for women." She explained that it puts men in a position of control and independence (men can open doors for themselves) and leaves her waiting helplessly for men do what she could do for herself. Like all rituals, opening doors is symbolic, and it conveys a cultural message: Men are active, capable, and independent, while women are passive, incapable, and dependent—yet another way to keep men in control.

The men roared back in a defensive chorus. "We aren't *trying* to dominate anyone," wrote one. "We're just being *polite.*"

"But," another woman objected, "there's more going on than the men admit." She pointed out that if this ritual were just performed out of politeness, *women* would also feel obliged to open doors for *men,* since being polite is something that runs both ways. Politeness, of course, can go in just one direction, as when subordinates defer to superiors.

"Well, maybe that's what door opening is," a man shot back. "Men are like servants waiting on women."

"But," came the swift reply, "if that were so, why is it so hard to get men to help us when we really need it? Why are we always stuck with the scut work at home and at work?"

It went on this way for quite a while, women objecting to *consequences* they didn't like and men defending against conscious *intentions* they didn't feel they had. The key to getting unstuck, I think, is to realize that consequences matter whether or not they're matched by intentions. "The road to hell," as the old saying goes, "is paved with good intentions." When men defend opening doors for women as just being polite, they assume it can't mean something they don't know about.

But what things mean isn't a private matter, because meaning comes from culture. Men can *think* they're just being nice guys, but that doesn't mean rushing ahead to open that door won't have social consequences beyond what they're aware of. In a patriarchal society, there's a good chance that the forms people follow—including being "polite"—are also patriarchal. In short, both sides of the argument can be right: Men may not consciously intend to put women down, and what men do often *does* put women down.

It's also worth noting that I didn't get the sense that the women in this conversation were trying to get the men to confess to some dark, malevolent motives. They weren't trying to make them feel bad about themselves or even apologize. What they were arguing for was for men to be conscious of what they were doing, to see how such patterns can produce bad consequences, and to do something to stop it.

Toward that end, it is generally useful to ask ourselves what we mean whenever we say, "I didn't mean it," because on some level, it's reasonable to assume that we mean everything we do and say. At a retirement party for a black manager, for example, a white colleague arranged a slide show that included pictures of black people happily eating watermelon. Blacks in the audience were shocked and angered, and when someone confronted the white man later on, his reaction was, "I'm not racist. I didn't mean anything by it."

In effect, "I didn't mean it" often comes close to "I didn't say it" or "I didn't do it," which of course isn't true. What, then, do the words signify? Most of the time, the real message is this: "I did it; I said it; but I didn't think about it." In many social situations, that kind of response clearly won't work. If I steal someone's car, the judge is unlikely to go easy on me if I say, "I didn't mean anything by it; I just wanted the car and I didn't think much about it at the time," or "I didn't consider whether the owner would mind," or "Getting arrested didn't cross my mind." The judge would probably say, "You *should* have thought about all those things." In other words, I'm held responsible to act with an ongoing awareness of the consequences of what I do and don't do.

But privilege works against such awareness in all kinds of social situations. The manager should have been mindful of racial patterns in mentoring and promotion. The white colleague should have thought about the cultural message behind demeaning stereotypes that associate blacks with watermelon. The man who sexually harassed should have been aware of what it's like to be a woman on the receiving end of such behavior. But they weren't, and such patterns are the norm, not the exception. Why?

If we use an individualistic model of the world, the answer is that people are callous or uncaring or prejudiced or too busy to bother with paying attention to their actions—especially if they're white or heterosexual or male. Sometimes, of course, this is true, but more often the larger truth is that the luxury of obliviousness makes a lack of conscious intent a path of least resistance that's easy to follow without knowing it. The sense of entitlement and superiority that underlies most forms of privilege runs so deep and is so entrenched that people don't have to think about it in order to act from it. They can always say they didn't mean it and, in a real sense, they're telling the truth. That's why "I didn't mean it" can be so disarming and such an effective way to defend privilege. They *weren't* thinking; they *weren't* mindful; they *weren't* aware—all the things that go into "meaning it." But this is precisely the problem with privilege and the damage that it does.

I'M ONE OF THE GOOD ONES

One way to acknowledge the problem of privilege and oppression and get off the hook at the same time is to make use of an illusion we looked at earlier: that bad things happen in social life simply because of bad people. Since I can make a good case that I'm not a bad person, then the trouble couldn't have anything to do with me.

"Racism still exists," I can say, "and it's a shame there are still bigots around like the Klan and the skinheads and neo-Nazis." Or "Unfortunately, some men still haven't gotten used to women in the workplace." Or "People who haven't worked through their homophobia make life difficult for gays and lesbians."

"And," I can hasten to add, if only to myself, "I don't belong to the Klan, I don't see color, I like women, and I have no 'problem' with gays and lesbians as far as I know."

Having set myself up as a good person with good intentions, I can feel disapproval or even compassion for all those bad, flawed, or sick people who supposedly make trouble happen all by themselves in spite of people like me. And I can sympathize with people who suffer as a result. But the issue of just where *I* am in all of this drops out of sight. Apparently I'm on the outside looking in as a concerned observer. I might even have moments when I count myself as a victim, since I feel bad whenever I think about it.

But the truth is that my silence, my inaction, and especially my passive acceptance of the everyday privilege that goes along with group membership are all it takes to make me just as much a part of the problem as any member of the Klan.

It's a point that's easy to miss, because we want people to see and judge us as individuals, not as members of a social category.[5] But when we insist on that, we're being naïve if not somewhat false, for the fact is that we *do* want people to treat us as members of social categories whenever it works to our advantage. When I go into a store, for example, I want to be waited on right away and treated with respect even though the clerks don't know a thing about me as an individual. I want them to accept my check or credit card and not treat me with suspicion and distrust. But all they know about me is the categories they think I belong to—a customer of a certain race, age, gender, and class—and all the things they think they know about people who belong to those categories. I want that to be enough. I don't want to have to prove over and over again that I'm someone who deserves to be trusted and taken seriously. I want them to *assume* all that, and the only way they can do that is to perceive me as belonging to the "right" social categories.

This is simply how social life works. By itself, it's not a problem. What many people resist seeing, however, is that on the other side of that same social process are all the people who get put into the "wrong" categories and ignored or followed around or treated with suspicion and disrespect regardless of who they are as individuals.

I can't have it both ways. If I'm going to welcome the way social categories work to my advantage, I also have to consider that when those same categories are used against others through no fault of their own, it then becomes *my* business because through that process *I* am being privileged at *their* expense.

In 1990, ABC News aired as a segment of *Prime Time* a documentary called *True Colors* that powerfully illustrates this dynamic. It focused on two men who were quite similar in every observable characteristic except race: one was black and one was white. The crew used hidden cameras and microphones to record what happened in various situations: applying for a job, accidentally locking yourself out of your car, trying to rent an apartment, shopping for shoes, buying a car, and so on. Over and over again the two men were treated differently. In one instance, the white man wandered into a shoe store in a shopping mall. He was barely across the threshold when the white clerk approached him with a smile and an outstretched hand. He looked at some shoes, and then went on his way. Minutes later his black partner entered the store and from the outset was utterly ignored by the clerk, who stood only a few feet away. Nothing the black man did seemed to make a difference. He picked up and looked at shoes, he walked up and down the display aisles, he gazed thoughtfully at a particular style. After what seemed an eternity, he left.

When I show *True Colors* in my race class and at diversity training sessions, I ask whites if they identify with anyone in the video. Invariably they say no, because they don't see themselves in the black man's predicament or in the racist behavior of the whites. Somehow, the white partner who is on the receiving end of preferential treatment is invisible to them, and if I don't mention him, he rarely comes up. In other words, they don't say, "Yes, I see myself in the white guy receiving the benefits of white privilege."

The effect of this obliviousness is for *them* to become invisible as white people in everyday situations and unaware of how privilege happens to them, especially in relation to other whites. They don't see themselves as being involved in situations where privilege comes into play. They don't see, for example, that simply being white puts them in a particular relationship with someone like the shoe store clerk (whom they readily identify as "racist"), or how this relationship results in the way black customers are treated and how *they* are treated as whites.

The invisibility of whiteness illustrates how privilege can blind those who receive it to what's going on. As Ruth Frankenberg writes about a white woman she interviewed, "Beth was much more sharply aware of racial *oppression* shaping Black experience than of race *privilege* shaping her own life. Thus, Beth could be alert to the realities of economic discrimination against Black communities while still conceptualizing her own life as racially neutral—nonracialized, nonpolitical."[6]

A common form of this is that women and racial minorities are often described as being treated unequally, but men and whites are not. This, however, is logically impossible. *Unequal* simply means "not equal," which describes both those who receive less than their fair share *and* those who receive more. But there can't be a short end of the stick without a long end, because it's the longness of the long end that makes the short end short. To pretend otherwise makes privilege and those who receive it invisible.

So long as we participate in a society that transforms difference into privilege, there is no neutral ground to stand on. If I'm in a meeting where men pay more attention to what I and other men say than to women, for example, I'm on the receiving end of privilege. My mere acceptance of that privilege— whether conscious or not—is all that other men need from me in order to perpetuate it. Other men *need* my compliance in order for sexist privilege to work, even if my compliance is unconscious and passive. I know this because as soon as I put more resistance around that path by speaking out and merely calling attention to it, I can feel the defensive response rise up to meet me. In this sense, I don't have to be consciously hostile toward women in order to play an integral role in maintaining male privilege as a pattern in this society.

In the same way, whites need the compliance of other whites in order for race privilege to work. If I look around my workplace and see no people of color, my silence on this issue sends the message to other whites that there *is* no issue. The shoe clerk's racist behavior depends on his being able to assume that other whites don't see a problem with preferential treatment for whites. That's what makes this path of racial preference a path of least resistance. And every white person either supports or challenges that assumption in choosing which path to follow. It is in the nature of social life that people continually look to one another to confirm or deny what they experience as reality. Given that, other people will interpret my going along with them down this path as my acceptance of that path unless I do something to make them think otherwise. Whether we know it or not, when someone discriminates by treating me better simply because I'm white, we walk down a path of racial privilege *together.*

There is no such thing as doing nothing. There is no such thing as being neutral or uninvolved. At every moment, social life involves each of us.

SICK AND TIRED

It's not unusual for whites to comment on how sick and tired they are of hearing about race. "It's always in your face," they say. I ask how often is "always," and what does "it" consist of? They become a bit vague. "Oh, it's in the news," they say, "all the time."

"Every day?" I ask.

"Well, it seems like it," they say.

"Every hour, every minute?"

"No, of course not," they say, and I can tell they're starting to get a little irritated with me. I realize they aren't trying to report an objective reality in the world. They're describing the feeling of being annoyed by something, put upon. When you're annoyed by something, it can seem as though it's everywhere, as if there's no escaping it. When it comes to the problem of privilege and oppression, privileged groups don't want to hear about it at all because it disturbs the luxury of obliviousness that comes with privilege. This means you don't have to bring it up very much in order for them to feel put upon. "Always" turns out to be somewhere between never and every minute. In reality, "all the time" comes down to "enough to make me look at what I don't want to look at, enough to make me uncomfortable." And usually that doesn't take much.

A similar dynamic operates with most forms of privilege. The middle and upper classes say they're sick and tired of hearing about welfare and poverty. Heterosexuals are sick and tired of hearing about gay and lesbian issues. And it takes almost no criticism at all in order for men to feel "bashed," like it's "open season on men." In fact, just saying "male privilege" or "patriarchy" can start eyes rolling and evoke that exasperated sense of "Here we go *again*."

In fact, 99 percent of the time there is utter silence in this society on the subject of gender privilege. In a system that privileges maleness, the default is *never* to do anything that might make men feel challenged or uncomfortable as men. In the same way, because whiteness is privileged over color, the norm is to never call attention to whiteness itself in ways that make white people uncomfortable. It's expected, of course, to routinely draw attention to male and white and heterosexual *people,* since our society is centered on and identified with those groups. But that differs from drawing attention to "male," "heterosexual," or "white" as social categories that are problematic.

Another reason for the "sick and tired" complaint is that life is hard for everyone. "Don't bring us your troubles," privileged groups say to the rest, "we've got troubles of our own." Many white men, for example, especially those who lack class privilege, spend a lot of time worrying about losing their jobs. So why should they have to listen to women or people of color talk about their problems with work, especially when the talk suggests that white men should be doing something more than they already are? When Marian Wright Edelman, founder and president of the Children's Defense Fund, says that it's "utterly exhausting being Black in America," many white people barely miss a beat in responding that they're tired, too.[7]

And of course, they are. They're exhausted from the pace of life that a competitive capitalist society imposes on everyone, and it's hard to hear about racism, sexism, and other forms of oppression. But it's one thing to have to hear about such problems and another to have to live them every day. The quick white defensiveness runs right past the fact that whatever it is that exhausts white people, it isn't the fact of being white. It may be exhausting to be a parent, or a worker, or a spouse, or a student who works all day and studies all night, but it's not exhausting to be a white person or, for that matter, a heterosexual or a man.

By comparison, blacks, women, and homosexuals have to do all the things that also exhaust whites, men, and heterosexuals, from raising families to earning a living to getting older. But on top of that, they must also struggle with the accumulation of fine grinding grit that oppression loads onto people's lives simply because they're in the "wrong" social category.

"I'm sick and tired" is a defense. It allows privileged groups to claim the protected status of victims. It reminds me of those times when a person injures you in some way, and when you confront them about it, they get angry at *you* because you've made them feel guilty about what they did. "Look how bad you've made me feel," they say, as if you're supposed to apologize for bringing your injury to their attention. Children often use this defense because they're so self-centered that the idea of taking responsibility for what they've done doesn't occur to them. When confronted with their misbehavior they sulk and glower and act hurt and put upon, as if someone has just laid a heavy and undeserved weight on their shoulders.

Privilege similarly encourages people to be self-centered and unaccountable to others. It encourages whites and men and other advantaged groups to behave as less than adults. It makes avoiding responsibility for what they do and don't do a path of least resistance. And yet, at the same time, these are the groups in charge of social institutions. People in these groups are the ones who occupy positions of responsible adult authority. It's a combination guaranteed to keep the trouble going unless the cycle of denial and defense is broken. The challenge for whites and men and heterosexuals is to see how privilege keeps them from growing up, how it diminishes everyone— including them—and blocks their potential to be part of the solution.

GETTING OFF THE HOOK
BY GETTING ON

If being on the hook for privilege and oppression means being perpetually vulnerable to guilt and blame, then we shouldn't be surprised that people do whatever they can to get off it. But according to my dictionary, *on the hook* also means being "committed," "obliged," and "involved."

In this sense, being on the hook is one of those things that distinguish adults from children—adults are and children aren't. When I'm on the hook, I feel called to use my power and authority as an adult to take responsibility, to act, to make things happen. Being "involved" makes me part of something larger, and I can't stand alone as an isolated individual. Being "obliged" means more than just being burdened, for it also connects me to people and makes me aware of how I affect them. And being "committed" to something focuses my potential to make a difference and bonds me to those who feel the same way.

Off the hook, I'm like a piece of wood floating with the current. On the hook, I have forward motion and a rudder to steer by. Off the hook, I live in illusion and denial, as if I can choose whether to be involved in the life of our society and the consequences it produces. But involvement is something that comes with being alive in the world as a human being. On the hook is where I can live fully in the world as it really is.

Trying to live off the hook puts members of privileged groups inside a tight little circle that cuts them off from much of what it means to be alive. They have to work to distance themselves from most of humanity, because they can't get close to other people without touching the trouble around privilege and oppression. Men living off the hook distance and insulate themselves from women, whites from people of color, heterosexuals from lesbians and gay men, the middle and upper classes from the working and lower classes. And the more diverse and interconnected the world becomes, the harder it is to sustain the illusion and the denial day after day, the more it takes to maintain the distance and deny the connection. They become like the person who loses the ability to feel pain, and bleeds to death from a thousand tiny cuts that go unnoticed, untreated, and unhealed.

Sooner or later, whites, heterosexuals, and men need to embrace this hook they're on, not as some terrible affliction or occasion for guilt and shame, but as a challenge and an opportunity. It's where they've been, where they are, and where they're going.

CHAPTER 10

What Can We Do?
Becoming Part of the Solution

The challenge we face is to change patterns of exclusion, rejection, privilege, harassment, discrimination, and violence that are everywhere in this society and have existed for hundreds (or, in the case of gender, thousands) of years. We have to begin by thinking about the trouble and the challenge in new and more productive ways as outlined in the preceding chapters. Here is a summary of the tools we have to start with.

Large numbers of people have sat on the sidelines and seen themselves as neither part of the problem nor the solution. Beyond this shared trait, however, they are far from homogeneous. Everyone is aware of the whites, heterosexuals, and men who intentionally act out in oppressive ways. But there is less attention to the millions of people who know inequities exist and want to be part of the solution. Their silence and invisibility allow the trouble to continue. Removing what silences them and stands in their way can tap an enormous potential of energy for change.

The problem of privilege and oppression is deep and wide, and to work with it we have to be able to see it clearly so that we can talk about it in useful ways. To do that, we have to reclaim some difficult language that names what's going on, language that has been so misused and maligned that it generates more heat than light. We can't just stop using words like *racism, sexism,* and *privilege,* however, because these are tools that focus our awareness on the problem and all the forms it takes. Once we can see and talk about what's going on, we can analyze how it works as a system. We can identify points of leverage where change can begin.

Reclaiming the language takes us directly to the core reality that the problem is privilege and the power that maintains it. Privilege exists when one group has something that is systematically denied to others not because of who they are or what they've done or not done, but because of the social category they belong to.

Privilege is a feature of social systems, not individuals. People have or don't have privilege depending on the system they're in and the social categories other people put them in. To say, then, that I have race privilege says less about me personally than it does about the society we all live in and how it is organized to assign privilege on the basis of a socially defined set of racial categories that change historically and often overlap. The challenge facing me as an individual has more to do with how I participate in society as a recipient of race privilege and how those choices oppose or support the system itself.

In dealing with the problem of privilege, we have to get used to being surrounded by paradox. Very often those who have privilege don't know it, for example, which is a key aspect of privilege. Also paradoxical is the fact that privilege doesn't necessarily lead to a "good life," which can prompt people in privileged groups to deny resentfully that they even have it. But privilege doesn't equate with being happy. It involves having what others don't have and the struggle to hang on to it at their

expense, neither of which is a recipe for joy, personal fulfill-
ment, or spiritual contentment.

For several centuries, capitalism has provided the economic
context for privilege and oppression based on difference. As
such, it has been and continues to be a powerful force, especially in relation to class, gender, and race. Its effects are both
direct and indirect. Historically, it was the engine that drove the
development of modern racism. In a less direct way, it creates
conditions of scarcity that set the stage for competition, fear,
and antagonism directed across differences of race, ethnicity,
and gender. Through the class differences that it creates, it also
shapes people's experience of privilege and the lack of it. This is
an example of the matrix of domination (or matrix of privilege)
through which the various forms of difference and privilege
interact and shape one another.

Difference takes many forms, but the most important are
those characteristics that are difficult or impossible to change
and that other people think they can identify just by looking
at someone. Oppression also takes many forms, most notably
avoidance, exclusion, rejection, unequal access to resources and
rewards, and violence. Just as privileged groups tend not to be
aware of privilege, they also tend not to be aware of how it happens from one moment to the next. Developing that ongoing
awareness is a key to becoming part of the solution.

Although disadvantaged groups take the brunt of the trouble, it also affects privileged groups. It does this in part because
misery visited on others comes back to haunt those who benefit
from it, especially in the form of defensiveness and fear. But it
also happens directly by limiting and shaping the lives of people
who receive privilege. Racism, for example, shapes both the
experience of being white and the experience of being a person
of color. The trouble also affects entire social systems, from organizations such as corporations and schools to communities,
societies, and global political and economic systems. In fact, it's
difficult to identify any aspect of social life that is left untouched

by systems of privilege and oppression. Being aware of this gives everyone a reason to include themselves in the solution, but it also gives us a clearer sense of how the trouble operates in the world and what we can do about it.

To be an effective part of the solution, we have to realize that privilege and oppression are not a thing of the past. It's happening right now. It isn't just a collection of wounds inflicted long ago that now need to be healed. The wounding goes on as I write these words and as you read them, and unless people work to change the system that promotes it, personal healing by itself cannot be the answer. Healing wounds is no more a solution to the oppression that causes the wounding than military hospitals are a solution to war. Healing is a necessary process, but it isn't enough.

The greatest barrier to change is that dominant groups don't see the trouble as *their* trouble, which means they don't feel obliged to do something about it. This happens for a variety of reasons: because they don't know the trouble exists in the first place, because they don't *have* to see it as their trouble, because they see it as a personal rather than a systemic problem, because they're reluctant to give up their privilege, because they feel angry and deprived and closed to the idea that they belong to privileged groups, because they're blinded by prejudice, because they're afraid of what will happen if they acknowledge the reality of privilege.

The two main approaches to change in organizations do little about these barriers. The "tin cup" approach and "business case" argument aren't powerful enough to engage men, heterosexuals, and whites over the long haul required for change. Those choices are the horns of the diversity dilemma on which most organizations find themselves today.

A third choice is to think about the trouble as everyone's responsibility—everybody's "hook"—and nobody's fault. This is especially difficult for members of privileged groups who have a hard time seeing themselves in relation to privilege without feeling guilty. It's easy to fall into this trap because people tend to use an individualistic model of the world that reduces everything to individual intentions and goodness or badness. A powerful and liberating alternative comes from the fact that we're always participating in something larger than ourselves: social systems. To understand racism, sexism, and other forms of trouble, we have to look at what we're participating in *and* how we choose to participate in relation to paths of least resistance.

This means we can be involved in a society's or organization's troubles without doing anything wrong and without being bad people. We don't have to think sexist or racist thoughts in order to participate in a system through which sexist and racist trouble happens. Participating is all it takes to involve us. It's also all it takes to give us the potential to be part of the solution, for when we see how we're connected to the problem, we can also see how we can make a difference by choosing differently as we participate in making systems happen.

Privilege is created and maintained through social systems that are dominated by, centered on, and identified with privileged groups. A racist society, for example, is white-dominated, white-centered, and white-identified. That doesn't mean it's full of people who feel animosity and malevolence toward people of color. The same can be said of any system that's racist—a church, a community, a corporation, a university. The systems are the "something larger than ourselves" that we participate in and that we have to understand in order to do something about the patterns of privilege that are part of how they work.

Since privilege is rooted primarily in systems—such as families, schools, and workplaces—change isn't simply a matter of changing people. People, of course, will have to change in order for systems to change, but the most important point is that changing people isn't enough. The solution also has to include entire systems such as capitalism whose paths of least resistance shape how we feel, think, and behave as individuals, how we see ourselves and one another.

As they work for change, it's easy for members of privileged groups to lose sight of the reality of privilege and its consequences and the truth that the trouble around privilege is their trouble as much as anyone else's. This happens in large part because systems of privilege provide endless ways of seeing and thinking about the world that make privilege invisible. These include denying and minimizing the trouble; blaming the victim; calling the trouble something else; assuming everyone prefers things the way they are; mistaking intentions with consequences; attributing the trouble to others and not their own participation in social systems that produce it; and balancing the trouble with troubles of their own. The more aware people can be of how these behaviors limit their effectiveness, the more they can contribute to change both in themselves and the systems where they work and live.

With these tools in hand, we can begin to think about how to make ourselves part of the solution to the problem of privilege and oppression. To do that, we first have to deal with some powerful myths about how change happens and how people can contribute to it.

MYTH 1: "IT'S ALWAYS BEEN THIS WAY, AND IT ALWAYS WILL"

If you don't make a point of studying history, it's easy to slide into the belief that things have always been the way we've known them to be. But if you look back a bit further, you find racial oppression has been a feature of human life for only a matter of centuries, and there is abundant evidence that male dominance has been around for only seven thousand years or so, which isn't very long when you consider that human beings have been on the earth for hundreds of thousands of years.[1] So when it comes to human social life, the smart money should be on the idea that *nothing* has always been this way or any other.

This idea should suggest that nothing *will* always be this way or any other, contrary to the notion that privilege and oppression are here to stay. If the only thing we can count on is change, then it's hard to see why we should believe for a minute that *any* kind of social system is permanent. Reality is always in motion. Things may appear to stand still, but that's only because humans have a short attention span, dictated perhaps by the shortness of our lives. If we take the long view—the *really* long view—we can see that everything is in process all the time.

Some would argue that everything *is* process, the space between one point and another, the movement from one thing toward another. What we may see as permanent end points— world capitalism, Western civilization, advanced technology, and so on—are actually temporary states on the way to other temporary states. Even ecologists, who used to talk about ecological balance, now speak of ecosystems as inherently unstable. Instead of always returning to some steady state after a period of disruption, ecosystems are, by nature, a continuing process of change from one arrangement to another. They never go back to just where they were.

Social systems are also fluid. A society isn't some hulking *thing* that sits there forever as it is. Because a system happens only as people participate in it, it can't help being a dynamic process of creation and re-creation from one moment to the next. In something as simple as a man following the path of least resistance toward controlling conversations (and a woman letting him do it), the reality of male privilege in that moment comes into being. This is how we *do* male privilege, bit by bit, moment by moment. This is also how individuals can contribute to change: by choosing paths of *greater* resistance, as when men don't take control and women refuse their own subordination.

Since people can always choose paths of greater resistance or create new ones entirely, systems can only be as stable as the flow of human choice and creativity, which certainly isn't a recipe for permanence. In the short run, systems of privilege may look unchangeable. But the relentless process of social life never produces the exact same result twice in a row, because it's impossible for everyone to participate in any system in an unvarying and uniform way. Added to this are the dynamic interactions that go on among systems—between capitalism and the state, for example, or between families and the economy—that also produce powerful and unavoidable tensions, contradictions, and other currents of change. Ultimately, systems can't help changing.

Oppressive systems often *seem* stable because they limit people's lives and imaginations so much that they can't see beyond them. But this masks a fundamental long-term instability caused by the dynamics of oppression itself. Any system organized around one group's efforts to control and exploit another is a losing proposition, because it contradicts the essentially uncontrollable nature of reality and does violence to basic human needs and values. For example, as the last two centuries of feminist thought and action have begun to challenge the violence and break down the denial, patriarchy has become increasingly vulnerable. This is one reason male resistance, backlash, and defensiveness are now so intense. Many men complain about their lot, especially their inability to realize ideals of control in relation to their own lives,[2] women, and other men. Fear of and resentment toward women are pervasive, from worrying about being accused of sexual harassment to railing against affirmative action.

No social system lasts forever, but this is especially true of oppressive systems of privilege. We can't know what will replace them, but we can be confident that they will go, that they *are* going at every moment. It's only a matter of how quickly, by what means, and toward what alternatives, and whether each of us will do our part to make it happen sooner rather than later and with less rather than more human suffering in the process.

MYTH 2: GANDHI'S PARADOX AND THE MYTH OF NO EFFECT

Whether we help change oppressive systems depends on how we handle the belief that nothing we do can make a difference, that the system is too big and powerful for us to affect it. The complaint is valid if we look at society as a whole: it's true that we aren't going to change it in our lifetime. But if changing the entire system through our own efforts is the standard against which we measure the ability to do something, then we've set ourselves up to feel powerless. It's not unreasonable to want to make a difference, but if we have to *see* the final result of what we do, then we can't be part of change that's too gradual and long term to allow that. We also can't be part of change that's so complex that we can't sort out our contribution from countless others that combine in ways we can never grasp. The problem of privilege and oppression requires complex and long-term change coupled with short-term work to soften some of its worst consequences. This means that if we're going to be part of the solution, we have to let go of the idea that change doesn't happen unless we're around to see it happen.

To shake off the paralyzing myth that we cannot, individually, be effective, we have to alter how we see ourselves in relation to a long-term, complex process of change. This begins by altering how we relate to time. Many changes can come about quickly enough for us to see them happen. When I was in college, for example, there was little talk about gender inequality as a social problem, whereas now there are more than five hundred women's studies programs in the United States. But a goal like ending oppression takes more than this and far more time than our short lives can encompass. If we're going to see ourselves as part of that kind of change, we can't use the human life span as a significant standard against which to measure progress.

To see our choices in relation to long-term change, we have to develop what might be called "time constancy," analogous to what psychologists call "object constancy." If you hold a cookie in front of very young children and then put it behind your back while they watch, they can't find the cookie because they apparently can't hold on to the image of it and where it went. They lack object constancy. In other words, if they can't see it, it might as well not even exist. After a while, children develop the mental ability to know that objects or people exist even when they're out of sight. In thinking about change and our relation to it, we need to develop a similar ability in relation to time that enables us to carry within us the knowledge, the faith, that significant change happens even though we aren't around to see it.

Along with time constancy, we need to clarify for ourselves how our choices matter and how they don't. Gandhi once said nothing we do as individuals matters, but that it's vitally important to do it anyway. This touches on a powerful paradox in the relationship between society and individuals. Imagine, for example, that social systems are trees and we are the leaves. No individual leaf on the tree matters; whether it lives or dies has no effect on much of anything. But collectively, the leaves are essential to the whole tree because they photosynthesize the sugar that feeds it. Without leaves, the tree dies.

So leaves matter and they don't, just as we matter and we don't. What each of us does may not seem like much, because in important ways, it *isn't* much. But when many people do this work together, they can form a critical mass that is anything but insignificant, especially in the long run. If we're going to be part of a larger change process, we have to learn to live with this sometimes uncomfortable paradox.

A related paradox is that we have to be willing to travel without knowing where we're going. We need faith to do what seems right without necessarily being sure of the effect that will have. We have to think like pioneers who may know the direction they want to move in or what they would like to find, without knowing where they will wind up. Because they are going where they've never been before, they can't know whether they will ever arrive at anything they might consider a destination, much less the kind of place they had in mind when they first set out. If pioneers had to know their destination from the beginning, they would never go anywhere or discover anything.

In similar ways, to seek out alternatives to systems of privilege it has to be enough to move away from social life organized around privilege and oppression and to move toward the certainty that alternatives are possible, even though we may not have a clear idea of what those are or ever experience them ourselves. It has to be enough to question how we see ourselves as people of a certain race, gender, class, and sexual orientation, for example, or examine how we see capitalism and the scarcity and competition it produces in relation to our personal striving to better our own lives, or how oppression works and how we participate in it. Then we can open ourselves to experience what happens next.

When we dare ask core questions about who we are and how the world works, things happen that we can't foresee; they don't happen unless we *move,* if only in our minds. As pioneers, we discover what's possible only by first putting ourselves in motion, because we have to move in order to change our position—and hence our perspective—on where we are, where we've been, and where we might go. This is how alternatives begin to appear.

The myth of no effect obscures the role we can play in the long-term transformation of society. But the myth also blinds us to our own power in relation to other people. We may cling to the belief that there is nothing we can do precisely because we subconsciously know how much power we *do* have and are afraid to use it because people may not like it. If we deny our power to affect people, then we don't have to worry about taking responsibility for how we use it or, more significant, how we don't.

This reluctance to acknowledge and use power comes up in the simplest everyday situations, as when a group of friends starts laughing at a racist, sexist, or homophobic joke and we have to decide whether to go along. It's just a moment among countless such moments that constitute the fabric of all kinds of oppressive systems. But it's a crucial moment, because the group's seamless response to the joke affirms the normalcy and unproblematic nature of it in a system of privilege. It takes only one person to tear the fabric of collusion and apparent consensus. On some level, we each know we have this potential, and this knowledge can empower us or scare us into silence. We can change the course of the moment with something as simple as visibly not joining in the laughter, or saying "I don't think that's funny." We know how uncomfortable this can make the group feel and how they may ward off their discomfort by dismissing, excluding, or even attacking us as bearers of bad news. Our silence, then, isn't because nothing we do will matter; our silence is our not *daring* to matter.

Our power to affect other people isn't simply the power to make them feel uncomfortable. Systems shape the choices people make primarily by providing paths of least resistance. Whenever we openly choose a different path, however, we make it possible for others to see both the path of least resistance they're following and the possibility of choosing something else.

If we choose different paths, we usually won't know if we're affecting other people, but it's safe to assume that we are. When people know that alternatives exist and witness other people choosing them, things become possible that weren't before. When we openly pass up a path of least resistance, we increase resistance for other people around that path, because now they must reconcile their choice with what they've seen us do, something they didn't have to deal with before. There's no way to predict how this will play out in the long run, but there's certainly no good reason to think it won't make a difference.

The simple fact is that we affect one another all the time without knowing it. When my family moved to our house in the woods of northwestern Connecticut, one of my first pleasures was blazing walking trails through the woods. Some time later I noticed deer scat and hoofprints along the trails, and it pleased me to think they had adopted the trail I'd laid down. But then I wondered if perhaps I had followed a trail laid down by others when I cleared "my" trail. I realized that there is no way to know that anything begins or ends with me and the choices I make. It's more likely that the paths others have chosen influence the paths I choose.

This suggests that the simplest way to help others make different choices is to make them myself, and to do it openly. As I shift the patterns of my own participation in systems of privilege, I make it easier for others to do so as well, and harder for them not to. Simply by setting an example—rather than trying to change them—I create the possibility of their participating in change in their own time and in their own way. In this way I can widen the circle of change without provoking the kind of defensiveness that perpetuates paths of least resistance and the oppressive systems they serve.

It's important to see that in doing this kind of work, we don't have to go after people to change their minds. In fact, changing people's minds may play a relatively small part in changing societies. We won't succeed in turning diehard misogynists into practicing feminists, for example, or racists into civil rights activists. At most, we can shift the odds in favor of new paths that contradict the core values that systems of privilege depend on. We can introduce so many exceptions to the paths that support privilege that the children or grandchildren of

diehard racists and misogynists will start to change their perception of which paths offer the least resistance. Research on men's
changing attitudes toward the male provider role, for example,
shows that most of the shift occurs *between* generations, not
within them.[3] This suggests that rather than trying to change
people, the most important thing we can do is contribute to the
slow evolution of entire cultures so that forms and values which
support privilege begin to lose their "obvious" legitimacy and
normalcy and new forms emerge to challenge their privileged
place in social life.

In science, this is how one paradigm replaces another.[4] For
hundreds of years, for example, Europeans believed that the
stars, planets, and sun revolved around Earth. But scientists such
as Copernicus and Galileo found that too many of their astro-
nomical observations were anomalies that didn't fit the prevailing paradigm: if the sun and planets revolved around the Earth,
then they wouldn't move as they did. As such observations accu-
mulated, they made it increasingly difficult to hang on to an
Earth-centered paradigm. Eventually the anomalies became so
numerous that Copernicus offered a new paradigm, which he
declined to publish for fear of persecution as a heretic, a fate
that eventually befell Galileo when he took up the cause a century later. Eventually, however, the evidence was so overwhelming that a new paradigm replaced the old one.

In similar ways, we can see how systems of privilege are
based on paradigms that shape how we think about difference
and how we organize social life in relation to it. We can openly
challenge those paradigms with evidence that they don't work
and produce unacceptable consequences for everyone. We can
help weaken them by openly choosing alternative paths in our
everyday lives and thereby provide living anomalies that don't
fit the prevailing paradigm. By our example, we can contradict
basic assumptions and their legitimacy over and over again. We
can add our choices and our lives to tip the scales toward new

paradigms that don't revolve around privilege and oppression. We can't tip the scales overnight or by ourselves, and in that sense we don't amount to much. But on the other side of Gandhi's paradox, it is crucial where we choose to place what poet Bonaro Overstreet called "the stubborn ounces of my weight":

STUBBORN OUNCES
(To One Who Doubts the Worth of Doing Anything
if You Can't Do Everything)

You say the little efforts that I make
will do no good; they will never prevail
to tip the hovering scale
where Justice hangs in balance.
      I don't think
I ever thought they would.
But I am prejudiced beyond debate
In favor of my right to choose which side
shall feel the stubborn ounces of my weight.[5]

It is in such small and humble choices that oppression and the movement toward something better actually happen.

STUBBORN OUNCES: WHAT CAN WE DO?

There are no easy answers to the question of what can we do about the problem of privilege. There is no twelve-step program, no neat set of instructions. Most important, there is no way around or over it: the only way out is through it. We won't end oppression by pretending it isn't there or that we don't have to deal with it.

Some people complain that those who work for social change are being "divisive" when they draw attention to gender or race or social class and the oppressive systems organized around them. But when members of dominant groups mark differences by excluding or discriminating against subordinate groups and treating them as "other," they aren't accused of being divisive. Usually it's only when someone calls attention to how differences are used for oppressive purposes that the charge of divisiveness comes up.

In a sense, it *is* divisive to say that oppression and privilege exist, but only insofar as it points to divisions that already exist and to the perception that the status quo is normal and unremarkable. Oppression promotes the worst kind of divisiveness because it cuts us off from one another and, by silencing us about the truth, cuts us off from ourselves as well. Not only must we participate in oppression by living in an oppressive society, we also must act as though oppression didn't exist, denying the reality of our own experience and its consequences for people's lives, including our own.

What does it mean to go out by going through? What can we do that will make a difference? I don't have the answers, but I do have some suggestions.

Acknowledge That the Trouble Exists

A key to the continued existence of every oppressive system is unawareness, because oppression contradicts so many basic human values that it invariably arouses opposition when people know about it. The Soviet Union and its East European satellites, for example, were riddled with contradictions so widely known among their people that the oppressive regimes fell apart with an ease and speed that astonished the world. An awareness of oppression compels people to speak out, to break the silence that continued oppression depends on.

This is why most oppressive cultures mask the reality of oppression by denying its existence, trivializing it, calling it something else, blaming it on those most victimized by it, or diverting attention from it. Instead of treating oppression as a serious problem, we go to war or get embroiled in controversial "issues" such as capital gains tax cuts or "family values" or immigrant workers. There would be far more active opposition to racism, for example, if white people lived with an ongoing awareness of how it actually affects the everyday lives of those it oppresses as "not white." As we have seen, however, the vast majority of white people *don't* do this.

It's one thing to become aware and quite another to stay that way. The greatest challenge when we first become aware of a critical perspective on the world is simply to hang on to it. Every system's paths of least resistance invariably lead away from critical awareness of how the system works. In some ways, it's harder and more important to pay attention to systems of privilege than it is to people's behavior and the paths of least resistance that shape it. As we saw earlier, for example, the structure of capitalism creates large social patterns of inequality, scarcity, and exploitation that have played and continue to play a major role in the perpetuation of racial, gender, and ethnic oppression. It is probably wishful thinking to suppose that we can end privilege and oppression without also changing a capitalist system of political economy that allows an elite to control the vast majority of wealth and income and leaves the rest of the population to fight over what's left. But such wishful thinking is, in fact, what we're encouraged to engage in most of the time—to cling to the idea that racism, for example, is just a problem with a few bad whites, rather than seeing how it is connected to a much larger matrix of privilege and oppression.

By not looking at the institutions through which humans organize economic and social life, we also engage in the fantasy that solving the problem of privilege and oppression is only a matter of changing how individual people think. I have, of course, spent most of this book talking about the importance of changing how we think about these issues, and I haven't suddenly changed my mind. We have for a long time been stuck in our ability to deal with these issues, and changing how we think is a key to getting unstuck.

By itself, however, changing how we think won't be enough to solve the problem. Oppression will not end simply as the result of a change in individual consciousness. Ultimately, we'll have to apply our understanding of how systems work to the job of changing systems themselves: economic, political, religious, educational, and familial. To return to my earlier discussion of the game of Monopoly, we have two choices if we don't like the consequences that result from playing it. One is to do what I did and stop. But since we don't have the option of not participating in our society, we're left with the second choice, which is to change the game itself.

Since there is a lot of resistance to following such paths, the easiest thing to do after reading a book like this is to forget about it. Maintaining a critical consciousness takes commitment and work; awareness is something we either maintain in the moment or we don't. And the only way to hang on to an awareness of systems of privilege is to make that awareness an ongoing part of our lives.

Pay Attention

Understanding how privilege and oppression operate and how you participate in them is where the work for change begins. It's easy to have opinions, but it takes work to know what you're talking about. The simplest way to begin is by reading, and making reading about privilege part of your life. Unless you have the luxury of a personal teacher, you can't understand this issue without reading, just as you'd need to read about a foreign country before you traveled there for the first time, or about a car before you tried to work under the hood. Many people assume they already know what they need to know because it's part of everyday life. But they're usually wrong. Just as the last thing a fish would discover is water, the last thing people discover is society itself and something as pervasive as the dynamics of privilege.

We also have to be open to the idea that what we think we know is, if not wrong, so deeply shaped by systems of privilege that it misses most of the truth. This is why activists talk with one another and spend time reading one another's writing: seeing things clearly is tricky. This is also why people who are critical of the status quo are so often self-critical as well: they know how complex and elusive the truth really is and what a challenge it is to work toward it. People working for change are often accused of being orthodox and rigid, but in practice they are typically among the most self-critical people around.

There is a huge literature on issues of difference available through any decent library system, although you'd never know it to judge from its invisibility in the mass media and mainstream bookstores. For that reason, it's a good idea not to rely on the media for meaningful analysis of social oppression. As large capitalist enterprises, the media have a vested interest in ignoring most of what is known about privilege, especially anything that seriously questions the status quo. Instead, they routinely focus on issues that have the least to do with privilege and oppression, that reflect the flawed individualistic models of social life, and that set subordinate groups against one another.

The media would rather discuss whether women and men have different brains, for example, than the reality of gender privilege and violence. And they are only too happy to give front-page coverage to any woman willing to criticize feminism, or any person of color willing to attack affirmative action or blame other people of color for their disadvantaged position in society. At the same time, they ignore most of what is known about oppression. Most feminist work, for example, is virtually invisible to book reviewers, journalists, editorial writers, columnists, and the audience for trade books. So if you want to know what's going on, it may take an interlibrary loan request or a special order at the bookstore. But you can do more than just request a book: you can tell librarians and bookstore managers how surprised and disappointed you are that they don't stock such essential reading for understanding the world we all have to live in.

As you educate yourself, it's important to avoid reinventing the wheel. Many people have already done a lot of work that you can learn from. There's no way to get through it all, but you don't have to in order to develop a clear enough sense of how to act in meaningful and informed ways. A good place to start is a basic text on race, class, and gender (these books increasingly include discussions of sexual orientation as well; see the Resources section of this book). Men who feel there is no place for them in women's studies might start with books about patriarchy and gender inequality that are written by men. In the same way, whites can begin with writings on race privilege written by other whites. Sooner or later, however, dominant groups will need to turn to what people in subordinate groups have written, because they are the ones who have done most of the work of figuring out how privilege and oppression operate.

Reading is only the beginning. At some point you have to look at yourself and the world to see if you can identify what you're reading about. Once the phrase "paths of least resistance" becomes part of your active vocabulary, for example, you start seeing them all over the place. The more aware you are of how powerful those paths are, the more easily you can decide whether to go down them each time they present themselves.

It helps to live like practicing anthropologists, participant-observers who watch and listen to other people and themselves, who notice patterns that come up again and again in social life. We can pretend we're strangers in a strange land who know nothing about where we are and *know* that we know nothing. This approach keeps us open to recognizing faulty assumptions and the surprise of realizing that things aren't what they seem. It is especially challenging for dominant groups, whose privilege tells them they shouldn't have to work to figure out someone else, that it's up to "others" to figure *them* out. It's easy for men, heterosexuals, and whites to fall into the trap of being like impatient, arrogant tourists who don't take the initiative to educate themselves about where they are. But taking responsibility means not waiting for others to tell you what to do, to point out what's going on, or to identify alternatives. If dominant groups are going to take their share of responsibility, it's up to them to listen, watch, ask, and listen again, to make it their business to find out for themselves. If they don't, they'll slide down the comfortable blindered path of privilege. And then they'll be *just* part of the problem and they *will* be blamed and they'll have it coming.

Little Risks: Do Something

The more you pay attention to privilege and oppression, the more you'll see opportunities to do something about them. You don't have to mount an expedition to find those opportunities; they're all over the place, beginning in yourself. As I became aware of how male privilege encourages me to control conversations, for example, I also realized how easily men dominate group meetings by controlling the agenda and interrupting, without women's objecting to it. This pattern is especially striking in groups that are mostly female but in which most of the talking nonetheless comes from a few men. I would find myself sitting in meetings and suddenly the preponderance of male voices would jump out at me, an unmistakable sign of male privilege in full bloom.

As I've seen what's going on, I've had to decide what to do about this little path of least resistance and my relation to it that leads me to follow it so readily. With some effort, I've tried out new ways of listening more and talking less. At times my methods have felt contrived and artificial, such as telling myself to shut up for a while or even counting slowly to ten (or more) to give others a chance to step into the space afforded by silence. With time and practice, new paths have become easier to follow and I spend less time monitoring myself. But awareness is never automatic or permanent, for paths of least resistance will be there to choose or not as long as male privilege exists.

As you become more aware, questions will arise about what goes on at work, in the media, in families, in communities, in religious institutions, in government, on the street, and at school—in short, just about everywhere. The questions don't come all at once (for which we can be grateful), although they sometimes come in a rush that can feel overwhelming. If you remind yourself that it isn't up to you to do it all, however, you can see plenty of situations in which you can make a difference, sometimes in surprisingly simple ways. Consider the following possibilities:

Make noise, be seen. Stand up, volunteer, speak out, write letters, sign petitions, show up. Every oppressive system feeds on silence. Don't collude in silence. Breaking the silence is especially important for dominant groups, because it undermines the assumption of solidarity that dominance depends on. If this feels too risky, you can practice being aware of how silence reflects your investment in solidarity with other dominant-group members. This can be a place to begin working on how you participate in making privilege and oppression happen: "Today I said nothing, colluded in silence, and this is how I benefited from it. Maybe tomorrow I can try something different."

Find little ways to withdraw support from paths of least resistance and people's choices to follow them, starting with yourself. It can be as simple as not laughing at a racist or heterosexist joke or saying you don't think it's funny, or writing a letter to your senator or representative or the editor of your newspaper, objecting to an instance of sexism in the media. When my local newspaper ran an article whose headline referred to sexual harassment as "earthy behavior," for example, I wrote a letter pointing out that harassment isn't "earthy."

The key to withdrawing support is to interrupt the flow of business as usual. We can subvert the assumption that we're all going along with the status quo by simply not going along. When we do this, we stop the flow, if only for a moment, but in that moment other people can notice and start to think and question. It's a perfect time to suggest the possibility of alternatives, such as humor that isn't at someone else's expense, or of ways to think about discrimination, harassment, and violence that do justice to the reality of what's going on and how it affects people.

People often like to think of themselves as individuals— especially in the United States. But it's amazing how much of the time we compare ourselves to other people as a way to see how well we fit in. Anything that disrupts this process in even the smallest way can affect taken-for-granted assumptions that underlie social reality. It might help to think of this process as inserting grains of sand in an oyster to irritate it into creating a pearl of insight; or as a way to make systems of privilege itch, stir, and scratch and thereby reveal themselves for others to see; or as planting seeds of doubt about the desirability and inevitability of the way things are and, by example, planting seeds of what might be.

Dare to make people feel uncomfortable, beginning with yourself. At the next local school board meeting, for example, you can ask why principals and other administrators are almost always white and male (unless your system is an exception that proves the rule), while the teachers they supervise are mostly women and people of color. Or look at the names and mascots used by local sports teams and see if they exploit the heritage and identity of Native Americans; if that's the case, ask principals and coaches and owners about it.[6] Consider asking similar kinds of questions about privilege and difference in your place of worship, workplace, and local government.

It may seem that such actions don't amount to much, until you stop for a moment and feel your resistance to doing them—worrying, for example, about how easily you could make people uncomfortable, including yourself. If you take that resistance to action as a measure of power, then your potential to make a difference is plain to see. The potential for people to feel uncomfortable is a measure of the power for change inherent in such simple acts of not going along with the status quo.

Some will say it isn't "nice" to make people uncomfortable, but oppressive systems do a lot more than make people feel uncomfortable, and there isn't anything "nice" about allowing that to continue unchallenged. Besides, discomfort is an unavoidable part of any meaningful process of education. We can't grow without being willing to challenge our assumptions and take ourselves to the edge of our competencies, where we're bound to feel uncomfortable. If we can't tolerate ambiguity, uncertainty, and discomfort, then we'll never get beneath superficial appearances or learn or change anything of much value, including ourselves.

And if history is any guide, discomfort—to put it mildly—is also an unavoidable part of changing systems of privilege. As sociologist William Gamson noted in his study of social movements, "the meek don't make it."[7] To succeed, movements must be willing to disrupt business as usual and make those in power as uncomfortable as possible. Women didn't win the right to vote, for example, by reasoning with men and showing them the merits of their position. To even get men's attention, they had to take to the streets in large numbers at considerable risk to themselves. At the very least they had to be willing to suffer ridicule and ostracism, but it often got worse than that. In England, for example, suffragettes were jailed and, when they went on hunger strikes, were force fed through tubes run down their throats. The modern women's movement has had to depend no less on the willingness of women to put themselves on the line in order to make men so uncomfortable that they've had to pay attention and, eventually, to act.

It has been no different with the civil rights movement. Under the leadership of men like Martin Luther King, the movement was dedicated to the principle of nonviolence. As with the movement for women's suffrage, however, they could get white people's attention only through mass demonstrations and marches. Whites typically responded with violence and intimidation.[8] As Douglas McAdam showed in his study of that period, the Federal government intervened and enacted civil rights legislation only when white violence against civil rights demonstrators became so extreme that the government was compelled to act.[9]

As the African American writer, orator, and abolitionist Frederick Douglass put it, "Power concedes nothing without a demand. It never has and it never will."[10] As much as anyone, I would like to believe Douglass is wrong, that all it takes to end an oppressive system is to point out the reality of oppression and the moral imperative that it not continue, and the receivers of privilege will somehow see the light and surrender their privilege without a fight. But history provides no reason to believe that to be true.

Openly choose and model alternative paths. As we identify paths of least resistance, we can identify alternatives and then follow them openly so that other people can see what we're doing. Paths of least resistance become more visible when people choose alternatives, just as rules become more visible when someone breaks them. Modeling new paths creates tension in a system, which moves toward resolution (like the irritated oyster). We don't have to convince anyone of anything. As Gandhi put it, the work begins with us as we try to be the change we want to see happen in the world. If you think this has no effect, watch how people react to the slightest departures from established paths and how much effort they expend trying to ignore or explain away or challenge those who choose alternative paths.

Actively promote change in how systems are organized around privilege. The possibilities here are almost endless, because social life is complicated and privilege is everywhere. You can, for example,

Speak out for equality in the workplace.

Promote diversity awareness and training.

Support equal pay and promotion.

Oppose the devaluing of women and people of color and the work they do, from dead-end jobs to glass ceilings.

Support the well-being of mothers and children and defend women's right to control their bodies and their lives.

Object to the punitive dismantling of welfare and attempts to limit women's access to reproductive health services.

Speak out against violence and harassment wherever they occur, whether at home, at work, or on the street.

Support government and private services for women who are victimized by male violence. Volunteer at the local rape crisis center or battered-women's shelter. Join and support groups that intervene with and counsel violent men.

Call for and support clear and effective anti-harassment policies in workplaces, unions, schools, professional associations, religious institutions, and political parties, as well as public spaces such as parks, sidewalks, and malls.

Object to theaters and video stores that carry violent pornography. This doesn't require a debate about censorship— just the exercise of freedom of speech to articulate pornography's role in the oppression of women and to express how its opponents feel about it.

Ask questions about how work, education, religion, and family are shaped by core values and principles that support race privilege, gender privilege, and other forms of privilege. You might accept women's entry into combat branches of the military or the upper reaches of corporate power as "progress," for example. But you could also raise questions about what happens to people and societies when political and economic institutions are organized around control, domination, "power over," and, by extension, competition and the use of violence. Is it progress to allow selected women to share control with men over oppressive systems?

Support the right of women and men to love whomever they choose. Raise awareness of homophobia and heterosexism. For example, ask school officials and teachers about what's happening to gay and lesbian students in local schools. If they don't know, ask them to find out, since it's a safe bet these students are being harassed, suppressed, and oppressed by others at one of the most vulnerable stages of life. When sexual orientation is discussed, whether in the media or among friends, raise questions about its relation to patriarchy. Remember that it isn't necessary to have answers to questions in order to ask them.

Pay attention to how different forms of oppression interact with one another. There has been a great deal of struggle within women's movements, for example, about the relationship between gender oppression and other forms of oppression, especially those based on race and social class. White middle- and upper-middle-class feminists have been criticized for pursuing their own agenda to the detriment of women who aren't privileged by class or race. Raising concerns about glass ceilings that keep women out of top corporate and professional positions, for example, does little to help working- or lower-class women. There has also been debate over whether some forms of oppression are more important to attack first or produce more oppressive consequences than other forms.

One way out of this conflict is to realize that patriarchy isn't problematic just because it emphasizes *male* dominance, but because it promotes dominance and control as ends in themselves. In that sense, all forms of oppression draw support from common roots, and whatever we do that calls attention to those roots undermines *all* forms of oppression. If working against patriarchy is seen simply as enabling some women to get a bigger piece of the pie, then some women probably will "succeed" at the expense of others who are disadvantaged by race, class, ethnicity, and other characteristics. One could make the same argument about movements for racial justice: If it just means enabling well-placed blacks to get ahead, then it won't end racial oppression for the vast majority. But if we identify the core problem as *any* society organized around principles of domination and privilege, then changing *that* requires us to pay attention to all the forms of oppression those principles promote. Whether we begin with race or gender or ethnicity or class or the capitalist system, if we name the problem correctly we'll wind up going in the same general direction.

Work with other people. This is one of the most important principles of participating in social change. From expanding consciousness to taking risks, being in the company of people who support what you're trying to do makes all the difference in the world. For starters, you can read and talk about books and issues and just plain hang out with other people who want to understand and do something about privilege and oppression. The roots of the modern women's movement were in consciousness-raising groups where women did little more than talk about themselves and try to figure out how they were shaped by a patriarchal society. It may not have looked like much at the time, but it laid the foundation for huge social change.

One step down this path is to share a book like this one with someone and then talk about it. Or ask around about local groups and organizations that focus on issues of difference and privilege; attend a meeting and introduce yourself to the members. After reading a book or article that you like, write to the author in care of the publisher (or, these days, send messages to web pages and email addresses). It's easy to think authors don't want to be bothered by interested readers, but the truth is, they usually welcome it and respond (I do!). Make contact; connect to other people engaged in the same work; do whatever reminds you that you're not alone in this.

It is especially important to form alliances across difference—for men to ally with women, whites with people of color, heterosexuals with lesbians and gay men. What does this mean? As Paul Kivel argues, one of the keys to being a good ally is a willingness to listen—for whites to listen to people of color, for example—and to give credence to what people say about their own experience.[11] This isn't easy to do, of course, since whites, heterosexuals, and men may not like what they hear about their privilege from those who are most damaged by it. It is difficult to hear anger about privilege and oppression and not take it personally, but that is what allies have to be willing to do. It's also difficult for members of privileged groups to realize how mistrusted they are by subordinate groups and to not take that personally as well. Kivel offers the following to give an idea of what people of color need from white allies (the same list could apply to allies across other forms of difference):

"respect"	"support"
"find out about us"	"listen"
"don't take over"	"don't make assumptions"
"provide information"	"stand by my side"
"resources"	"don't assume you know
"money"	what's best for me"
"take risks"	"put your body on the line"
"don't take it personally"	"make mistakes"
"understanding"	"honesty"
"teach your children about	"talk to other white people"
racism"	"interrupt jokes and
"speak up"	comments"
"don't be scared of my	"don't ask me to speak for
anger"	my people"

One of the most important items on Kivel's list is for whites to talk to other white people. In many ways, the biggest challenge for members of privileged groups is to work with one another on issues of privilege rather than trying to help members of subordinate groups. Perhaps the biggest thing that men can do against sexism, for example, is to educate other men about patriarchy and confront other men about sexist behavior and the reality of male privilege. The same can be said about whites in relation to racism and straights in relation to heterosexism. For members of privileged groups to become allies, they must recall Frederick Douglass's words, that "power concedes nothing without a demand," and add their weight to that demand. When whites work against white privilege, when heterosexuals act against heterosexual privilege, and when men act against male privilege, they do more than add their voices. They also make it more difficult for other members of privileged groups to dismiss calls for change as simply the actions of "special interest groups" trying to better their position.

Speaking out is, of course, a hard and risky thing to do, because receiving privilege depends on being accepted by other members of the privileged group. But it is not possible to both work to end privilege and hang on to it at the same time.

Don't keep it to yourself. A corollary of looking for company is not to restrict your focus to the tight little circle of your own life. It isn't enough to work out private solutions to social problems like oppression and keep them to yourself. It isn't enough to clean up your own act and then walk away, to find ways to avoid the worst consequences of oppression and privilege at home and inside yourself and think that's taking responsibility. Privilege and oppression aren't a personal problem that can be solved through personal solutions. At some point, taking responsibility means acting in a larger context, even if that means letting just one other person know what you're doing. It makes sense to start with yourself, but it's equally important not to end with yourself.

A good way to convert personal change into something larger is to join an organization dedicated to changing the systems that produce privilege and oppression. Most college and university campuses, for example, have student organizations that focus on issues of gender, race, and sexual orientation. There are also national organizations working for change, often through local and statewide branches. Consider, for example, the National Organization for Women (NOW), the National Association for the Advancement of Colored People (NAACP), the National Conference for Community and Justice (formerly the National Conference of Christians and Jews), the National Gay and Lesbian Task Force, the Southern Poverty Law Center, the National Organization of Men Against Sexism, the Feminist Majority, the National Abortions Rights Action League, the Southern Christian Leadership Conference, and the National Urban League.

If all this sounds overwhelming, remember again that we don't have to deal with everything. We don't have to set ourselves the impossible task of transforming society or even ourselves. All we can do is what *we* can *manage* to do, secure in the knowledge that we're making it easier for other people—now and in the future—to see and do what *they* can do. So, rather than defeat ourselves before we start: Think small, humble, and doable rather than large, heroic, and impossible. Don't paralyze yourself with impossible expectations. It takes very little to make a difference. Small acts can have radical implications. If the main requirement for the perpetuation of evil is that good people do nothing, then the choice isn't between all or nothing, but between nothing and *something*.

Don't let other people set the standard for you. Start where you are and work from there. Make lists of all the things you could actually imagine *doing*—from reading another book about inequality to suggesting policy changes at work to protesting against capitalism to raising questions about who cleans the bathroom at home—and rank them from the most risky to the least. Start with the least risky and set reasonable goals ("What small risk for change will I take *today?*"). As you get more experienced at taking risks, you can move up your list. You can commit yourself to whatever the next steps are for you, the tolerable risks, the contributions that offer some way—however small it might seem—to help balance the scales. As long as you do something, it counts.

In the end, taking responsibility doesn't have to involve guilt and blame, letting someone off the hook, or being on the hook yourself. It simply means acknowledging an obligation to make a contribution to finding a way out of the trouble we're all in, and to find constructive ways to act on that obligation. You don't have to do anything dramatic or earth-shaking to help change happen. As powerful as oppressive systems are, they cannot stand the strain of lots of people doing something about it, beginning with the simplest act of naming the system out loud.

WHAT'S IN IT FOR ME?

It's risky to promote change. You risk being seen as odd, being excluded or punished for asking questions and setting examples that make people uncomfortable or threaten privilege. We've all adapted in one way or another to life in a society organized around competition, privilege, and difference. Paths of least resistance may perpetuate oppression, but they also have the advantage of being familiar and predictable and therefore can seem preferable to untried alternatives and the unknown. There are inner risks—of feeling lost, confused, and scared— along with outer risks of being rejected or worse. Obviously, then, working for change isn't a path of least resistance, which raises the question of why anyone should follow Gandhi's advice and do it anyway.

It's an easier question to answer for subordinate groups than it is for dominants, which helps explain why the former have done most of the work for change. Those on the losing end have much to gain by striving to undo the system that oppresses them, not only for themselves in the short run, but for the sake of future generations. The answer comes less easily for those in dominant groups, but they don't have to look very far to see that they have much to gain—especially in the long run—that more than balances what they stand to lose.[12]

When whites, heterosexuals, and men join the movement against privilege and oppression, they can begin to undo the costs of participating in an oppressive system as the dominant group. Few men, for example, realize how much they deaden themselves in order to support (if only by their silence) a system that privileges them at women's expense, that values maleness by devaluing femaleness, that makes women invisible in order to make men appear larger than life. Most men don't realize the impoverishment to their emotional and spiritual lives, the price they pay in personal authenticity and integrity, how they compromise their humanity, how they limit the connections they can have with other people, how they distort their sexuality to live up to core patriarchal values of control. They don't realize how much they have to live a lie in order to interact on a daily basis with their mothers, wives, sisters, daughters, women friends and coworkers—all members of the group male privilege oppresses. So the first thing men can do is claim a sense of aliveness and realness that doesn't depend on superiority and control, and a connection to themselves and the world—which they may not even realize was missing until they begin to feel its return.

In similar ways, most whites don't realize how much energy it takes to defend against their continuing vulnerability to guilt and blame and to avoid seeing how much trouble the world is in and the central role they play in it. When whites do nothing about racial privilege and oppression, they put themselves on the defensive, in the no-safe-place-to-hide position of every dominator class. But when white people make a commitment to participate in change, to be more than part of the problem, they free themselves to live in the world without feeling open to guilt simply for being white.

In perhaps more subtle ways, homophobia and heterosexism take a toll on heterosexuals. The persecution of lesbians, for example, is a powerful weapon of sexism that encourages women to silence themselves, to disavow feminism, and tolerate male privilege for fear that if they speak out, they'll be labeled as lesbians and ostracized.[13] In similar ways, the fear of being called gay is enough to make men conform to masculine stereotypes that don't reflect who they really are and to go along with an oppressive gender system they may not believe in. And because homosexuals all come from families, parents and siblings may also pay a huge emotional price for the effects of prejudice, discrimination, and persecution directed at their loved ones.

With greater authenticity and aliveness comes the opportunity to go beyond the state of arrested development, the perpetual adolescence that privilege promotes in dominant groups, to move away from unhealthy dependencies on the subordination and undervalued labor of others and toward healthy interdependencies free of oppressive cultural baggage.

When people join together to end any form of oppression, they act with courage to take responsibility to do the right thing, and this empowers them in ways that can extend to every corner of their lives. Whenever we act with courage, a halo effect makes that same courage available to us in other times and places. When we step into our legacies and take responsibility for them, we can see how easily fear keeps us from acting for change in ourselves and in the systems we participate in. As we do the work, we build a growing store of experience to draw on in figuring out how to act with courage again and again. As our inner and outer lives become less bound by the strictures of fear and compromise, we can claim a deeper meaning for our lives than we've known before.

The human capacity to choose how to participate in the world empowers all of us to pass along something different from what's been passed to us. With each strand of the knot of privilege that we help to work loose and unravel, we don't act simply for ourselves, we join a process of creative resistance to oppression that's been unfolding for thousands of years. We become part of the long tradition of people who have dared to make a difference—to look at things as they are, to imagine something better, and to plant seeds of change in themselves, in others, and in the world.

Acknowledgments

As this book goes to press, I'm mindful of people who have played an important part in the work that led to the writing of it. My thanks go to my sister, Annalee Johnson, who introduced me to training work around issues of difference and encouraged me to take a chance. I'm especially grateful to my friend and colleague Jane Tuohy (to whom this book is dedicated) who more than anyone else has provided me with a vision of how I might use what I know in nonacademic settings, along with countless opportunities to do so. She has been a role model, a source of affirmation and support, and, at times, a worthy and thoughtful adversary in the heated discussions through which we continue to work through our understanding of these difficult issues as they play out in the real world of people's lives.

I'm also grateful to Shirley Harrell, Ed Hudner, Deat LaCour, Larry Mack, Robin Brown-Manning, and Helen Turnbull for all that I've learned in working with them, and to Leslie Brett, Kim Cromwell, Carolyn Gabel, and Anne Menard for how effectively they model lives dedicated to change. I'm especially grateful to my Race in America teaching partner, Fredrica Gray, for her strength and wisdom, her extraordinary breadth of knowledge, and her unfailing sense of humor when we've needed it most.

I give my thanks for the thoughtful feedback and suggestions offered by the several reviewers of the manuscript including Leon F. Burrell, University of Vermont; Joan L. Griscom, William Paterson University; Betsy Lucal, Indiana University, South Bend; Tracy Ore, Saint Cloud State University; Fred L. Pincus, University of Maryland, Baltimore County; Sherwood Smith, University of Vermont; and Robert L. Walsh, University of Vermont. I'm especially thankful to Estelle Disch, University of Massachusetts, Boston; Paula Rothenberg, William Paterson University; and Michael Schwalbe, North Carolina State University, for challenging me in all the right places.

I thank the wonderful editorial and production crew at Mayfield Publishing Company. I thank my editor, Serina Beauparlant not only for her support and encouragement, but for what have been perhaps the most interesting and creative marathon phone calls I've ever had. I thank my copy editor Anne Montague for helping with problems I was having difficulty resolving on my own, and thank Julianna Scott Fein, production editor, for expertly guiding the manuscript into print. I would also like to thank the other members of the production team: Violeta Díaz, design manager; Robin Mouat, art editor; Linda Robertson, text designer; and Joan Greenfield, cover designer.

My deepest gratitude is reserved for my comrade, soul mate, and partner in life, Nora L. Jamieson, for all that she does to nurture and challenge and support the writer in me, for all the moments when she has held the vision I'd lost sight of, and for the example of her own courage and wisdom in the face of a world in desperate need of both.

Notes

CHAPTER 3: THE TROUBLE WE'RE IN

1. "White, Male, and Worried," *Business Week*, January 31, 1994, p. 55.
2. Marilyn Loden and Judy B. Rosener, *Workforce America: Managing Employee Diversity as a Vital Resource* (Homewood, Ill.: Business One Irwin, 1991), p. 20.
3. The sections that follow are organized around types of behavior that are discussed in terms of racism by Joe R. Feagin and Melvin P. Sikes, *Living with Racism: The Black Middle-Class Experience* (Boston: Beacon Press, 1994), pp. 21–22. I apply them more broadly.
4. James Baldwin, "On Being 'White' . . . and Other Lies," *Essence*, 1984. Reprinted in David R. Roediger (ed.), *Black on White: Black Writers on What It Means to Be White*, pp. 177–80 (New York: Schocken Books, 1999).
5. For more on the social construction of whiteness, see Theodore W. Allen, *The Invention of the White Race*, vol. 1: *Racial Oppression and Social Control* (New York: Verso, 1994); vol. 2: *The Origin of Racial Oppression in Anglo-America* (New York: Verso, 1997); Charles Gallagher, "White Racial Formation: Into the Twenty-First Century," in Richard Delgado and Jean Stefancic (eds.), *Critical White Studies* (Philadelphia: Temple University Press, 1997), pp. 6–11; Christopher Wills, "The Skin We're In," in Delgado and Stefancic, pp. 12–14; Reginald Horsman, "Race and Manifest Destiny: The Origins of American Racial Anglo-Saxonism," in Delgado and Stefancic, pp. 139–44; and Kathleen Neal Cleaver, "The Antidemocratic Power of Whiteness," in Delgado and Stefancic, pp. 157–63.
6. For her now classic statement on the concept of privilege, see Peggy McIntosh, "White Privilege and Male Privilege: A Personal Account of Coming to See Correspondences Through Work in Women's Studies." Widely reprinted, it can be found in Anne Minas (ed.), *Gender Basics: Feminist Perspectives on Women and Men* (Belmont, Calif.: Wadsworth, 1993), pp. 30–38.
7. Ibid., p. 35.
8. Robert Terry, "The Negative Impact of White Values," in Benjamin P. Bowser and Raymond Hunt (eds.), *Impacts of Racism on White Americans* (Newbury Park, Calif.: Sage Publications, 1981), p. 120.
9. Ellis Cose, *Rage of a Privileged Class* (New York: HarperCollins, 1993), p. 48.
10. Much of what follows is drawn from Joseph Barndt, *Dismantling Racism: The Continuing Challenge to White America* (Minneapolis:

Augsburg, 1991); Cose, *Rage of a Privileged Class;* Feagin and Sikes, *Living with Racism;* Paul Kivel, *Uprooting Racism: How White People Can Work for Racial Justice* (Philadelphia: New Society Publishers, 1996); McIntosh, "White Privilege and Male Privilege"; and David T. Wellman, *Portraits of White Racism,* 2nd ed. (New York: Cambridge University Press, 1993).

11. Kivel, *Uprooting Racism,* p. 112.
12. See Ruth Frankenberg, *The Social Construction of Whiteness: White Women, Race Matters* (Minneapolis: University of Minnesota Press, 1993).
13. Charlotte Bunch, "Not for Lesbians Only," *Quest* 11, no. 2 (Fall 1975).
14. Harry Brod, "Work Clothes and Leisure Suits: The Class Basis and Bias of the Men's Movement," in Michael Kimmel and Michael A. Messner (eds.), *Men's Lives* (New York: Macmillan, 1989), p. 280. Italics in original.
15. For a classic discussion of the meaning of oppression, see Marilyn Frye, *The Politics of Reality: Essays in Feminist Theory* (Trumansburg, N.Y.: Crossing Press, 1983), pp. 1–16.

CHAPTER 4: CAPITALISM, CLASS, AND THE MATRIX OF DOMINATION

1. If you want to know more about this, two good basic sources are Richard C. Edwards, Michael Reich, and Thomas E. Weisskopf, *The Capitalist System,* 3rd ed. (Englewood Cliffs, N.J.: Prentice-Hall, 1986), and Joan Smith, *Social Issues and the Social Order: The Contradictions of Capitalism* (Cambridge, Mass.: Winthrop, 1981). See also Peter Saunders, *Capitalism* (Minneapolis: University of Minnesota Press, 1995). And for a more whimsical (but no less informative) view, try David Smith and Phil Evans, *Marx's "Kapital" for Beginners* (New York: Pantheon, 1982).
2. "House Passes Physician Bargaining Bill," *Reuter's Online,* June 30, 2000.
3. See Charles C. Ragin and Y. W. Bradshaw, "International Economic Dependence and Human Misery: 1938–1980: A Global Perspective," *Sociological Perspectives* 35(2), 1992, pp. 217–47. See also Harold R. Kerbo, *Social Stratification and Inequality,* 4th ed. (New York: McGraw-Hill, 1999), chapter 13.
4. Joint Economic Committee, *The Concentration of Wealth in the United States* (Washington, D.C.: Joint Economic Committee of the U.S. Congress, 1986). See also Fred Brock, "The Richer Rich and Where

They Live," *New York Times*, April 19, 1998; Barbara Crossette, "Worldwide, Most Are Consuming More, and the Rich Much More," *New York Times*, September 13, 1998; and David R. Francis, "Where Did All The Money Go? Not Far," *Christian Science Monitor*, July 16, 1997.

5. U.S. Census Bureau, *Current Population Reports, Series P60-206, Money Income in the United States, 1998* (Washington, D.C.: U.S. Government Printing Office, 1999), p. xiii.

6. For more on class, see Kerbo, *Social Stratification*, chapters 6–9, and E. O. Wright, *Classes* (New York: Schocken, 1985).

7. See, for example, Leonard Beeghley, *Living Poorly in America: The Reality of Poverty and Pauperism* (New York: Praeger, 1983); Frances Fox Piven and Richard A. Cloward, *Regulating the Poor: The Functions of Public Welfare*, updated edition (New York: Vintage Books, 1993); and Jeffrey Reiman, *The Rich Get Richer and the Poor Get Prison: Ideology, Class, and Criminal Justice*, 6th ed. (New York: Macmillan, 2000).

8. See, for example, Martha R. Burt, *Over the Edge: The Growth of Homelessness in the 1980s* (New York: Russell Sage Foundation, 1992); and Peter H. Rossi, *Down and Out in America: The Origins of Homelessness* (Chicago: University of Chicago Press, 1989).

9. For more on this, see Kerbo, *Social Stratification*, chapter 11.

10. See Sheldon Danziger and Peter Gottschalk, *Uneven Tides: Rising Inequality in America* (New York: Russell Sage Foundation, 1993).

11. These figures come from General Social Survey data provided by the University of Chicago's National Opinion Research Center. James A. Davis and Tom W. Smith, *General Social Surveys, 1972–1996: Cumulative Code Book.*

12. See, for example, Barbara Ehrenreich, *Fear of Falling: The Inner Life of the Middle Class* (New York: HarperCollins, 1989); and Juliet B. Schor, *The Overworked American: The Unexpected Decline of Leisure* (New York: Basic Books, 1993).

13. Lester C. Thurow, *The Zero-Sum Society: Distribution and the Possibilities for Economic Change* (New York: Basic Books, 1980).

14. U.S. Census Bureau, *Negro Population: 1790–1915* (Washington, D.C.: U.S. Government Printing Office, 1918).

15. See Theodore W. Allen, *The Invention of the White Race*, vol. 1: *Racial Oppression and Social Control*, and vol. 2: *The Origin of Racial Oppression in Anglo-America* (New York: Verso, 1994, 1997).

16. For a vivid description and analysis of this, see W. E. B. Du Bois, *The Souls of Black Folk* (New York: Penguin, 1989), chapter 8.

17. See Ronald Takaki, *Iron Cages: Race and Culture in 19th-Century America* (New York: Oxford, 1979) and *Strangers from a Different Shore* (New York: Penguin, 1989).

18. See the following by Immanuel Wallerstein: *The Modern World System* (New York: Academic Press, 1976); *The Capitalist World-Economy* (Cambridge: Cambridge University Press, 1979); *The Modern World System II: Mercantilism and the Consolidation of the European World Economy, 1600–1750* (New York: Academic Press, 1980); *The Modern World System III: The Second Era of Great Expansion of the Capitalist World-Economy, 1730–1840* (New York: Academic Press, 1989). See also Howard Zinn, *A People's History of the United States*, 20th anniv. ed. (New York: HarperCollins, 1999).

19. See Dee Brown, *Bury My Heart at Wounded Knee: An Indian History of the American West* (New York: Henry Holt, 1991).

20. See Allen, *Racial Oppression and Social Control* and *The Origin of Racial Oppression in Anglo-America,* Charles Gallagher, "White Racial Formation: Into the Twenty-First Century," in Richard Delgado and Jean Stefancic, eds., *Critical White Studies,* pp. 6–11 (Philadelphia: Temple University Press, 1997); Kathleen Neal Cleaver, "The Antidemocratic Power of Whiteness," in Delgado and Stefancic, pp. 157–63; Baldwin, "On Being 'White' . . . and Other Lies."

21. See Reginald Horsman, "Race and Manifest Destiny: The Origins of American Racial Anglo-Saxonism," in Delgado and Stefancic, pp. 139–44.

22. See David R. Roediger, *The Wages of Whiteness: Race and the Making of the American Working Class* (London and New York: Verso, 1991).

23. A powerful example of a situation in which this strategy ultimately failed is the great coal mine strike early in the twentieth century dramatized in the film *Matewan.*

24. See, for example, Heidi I. Hartmann, "The Family as the Locus of Gender, Class, and Political Struggle: The Example of Housework," *Signs: Journal of Women in Culture and Society* 6 (Spring 1981), pp. 366–94; and Eli Zaretsky, *Capitalism, the Family, and Personal Life* (New York: Harper & Row, 1986).

25. See Barbara Reskin, "Bringing the Men Back In: Sex Differentiation and the Devaluation of Women's Work," *Gender and Society* 2, no. 1 (March 1988); and Irene Tinker, *Persistent Inequalities: Women and World Development* (New York: Oxford, 1990).

26. See Marilyn Waring, *If Women Counted: A New Feminist Economics* (San Francisco: HarperCollins, 1988).

27. See Patricia Hill Collins, *Black Feminist Thought: Knowledge, Consciousness, and the Politics of Empowerment* (New York: Routledge, 1991), chapter 11; Estelle Disch, *Reconstructing Gender: A Multicultural Anthology* (Mountain View, Calif.: Mayfield, 1997), p. 6. See also bell hooks, *Talking Back: Thinking Feminist, Thinking Black* (Boston: South End Press, 1989); Judith Lorber, *Paradoxes of Gender* (New Haven, Conn.: Yale University Press, 1995); Audre Lorde,

Sister Outsider: Essays and Speeches (Freedom, Calif.: Crossing Press, 1984), especially pp. 114–23; and Gerda Lerner, "Reconceptualizing Differences Among Women," in Alison M. Jagger and Paula S. Rothenberg (eds), *Feminist Frameworks*, 3rd ed. (New York: McGraw-Hill, 1993), pp. 237–48.

28. See Ronald Takaki, *Strangers from a Different Shore: A History of Asian-Americans* (Boston: Little, Brown, 1989), p. 474.
29. See Kivel, *Uprooting Racism*, pp. 136, 137, 138.

CHAPTER 5: MAKING PRIVILEGE HAPPEN

1. See John F. Dovidio and Samuel L. Gaertner (eds.), *Prejudice, Discrimination, and Racism* (Orlando, Fla.: Academic Press, 1986).
2. The classic work on prejudice is Gordon W. Allport, *The Nature of Prejudice* (New York: Anchor Books, 1958). See also Dovidio and Gaertner, *Prejudice, Discrimination, and Racism,* and Daniela Gioseffi (ed.), *On Prejudice: A Global Perspective* (New York: Anchor Books, 1993).
3. There is a huge body of literature on the costs of privilege to women, homosexuals, and racial and ethnic minorities. See, for example, Joan Abramson, *Old Boys—New Women: Sexual Harassment in the Workplace* (New York: Praeger, 1993); American Association of University Women, *How Schools Shortchange Girls* (Washington, D.C.: American Association of University Women, 1992); Derrick Bell, *And We Are Not Saved: The Elusive Quest for Racial Justice* (New York: Basic Books, 1987); Derrick Bell, *Faces at the Bottom of the Well: The Permanence of Racism* (New York: Basic Books, 1992); Lois Benjamin, *The Black Elite: Facing the Color Line in the Twilight of the Twentieth Century* (Chicago: Nelson-Hall, 1991); Center for Research on Women, *Secrets in Public: Sexual Harassment in Our Schools* (Wellesley, Mass.: Wellesley College Center for Research on Women, 1993); Kim Chernin, *The Obsession: Reflections on the Tyranny of Slenderness* (New York: Harper & Row, 1981); David Gary Comstock, *Violence Against Lesbians and Gay Men* (New York: Columbia University Press, 1991); Cose, *Rage of a Privileged Class;* Angela Y. Davis, *Women, Race, and Class* (New York: Random House, 1981); Andrea Dworkin, *Woman Hating* (New York: Dutton, 1974); Barbara Ehrenreich and Deidre English, *For Her Own Good: 150 Years of Experts' Advice to Women* (New York: Anchor Books, 1978); Cynthia Fuchs Epstein, *Deceptive Distinctions: Sex, Gender, and the Social Order* (New Haven, Conn.: Yale University Press, 1989); Susan Faludi, *Backlash: The Undeclared War Against American Women* (New York: Crown, 1991); Feagin and Sikes,

Living with Racism; Marilyn French, *Beyond Power: On Men, Women, and Morals* (New York: Summit Books, 1985); Marilyn French, *The War Against Women* (New York: Summit Books, 1992); Carol Brooks Gardner, *Passing By: Gender and Public Harassment* (Berkeley: University of California Press, 1995); Andrew Hacker, *Two Nations: Black and White, Separate, Hostile, Unequal* (New York: Scribner, 1992); Arlie Hochschild, *The Second Shift: Working Parents and the Revolution at Home* (New York: Viking/Penguin, 1989); bell hooks, *Ain't I a Woman: Black Women and Feminism* (Boston: South End Press, 1981); bell hooks, *Feminist Theory: From Margin to Center* (Boston: South End Press, 1984); hooks, *Talking Back;* bell hooks, *Sisters of the Yam: Black Women and Self-Recovery* (Boston: South End Press, 1993); Fran P. Hosken, *The Hosken Report: Genital and Sexual Mutilation of Females,* 4th rev. ed. (Lexington, Mass.: Women's International Network News, 1994); Kivel, *Uprooting Racism;* Laura Lederer, (ed.), *Take Back the Night: Women on Pornography* (New York: Morrow, 1980); Lorber, *Paradoxes of Gender;* Lorde, *Sister Outsider;* Catharine A. MacKinnon, *Only Words* (Cambridge, Mass.: Harvard University Press, 1993); Brian McNaught, *Gay Issues in the Workplace* (New York: St. Martin's Press, 1993); Cherríe Moraga and Gloria Anzaldúa (eds.), *This Bridge Called My Back: Writings by Radical Women of Color* (New York: Kitchen Table: Women of Color Press, 1983); Michele A. Paludi, *Ivory Power: Sexual Harassment on Campus* (Albany: State University of New York Press, 1990); Suzanne Pharr, *Homophobia: A Weapon of Sexism* (Inverness, Calif.: Chardon Press, 1988); Adrienne Rich, *Of Woman Born* (New York: Norton, 1976); Diana E. H. Russell, *Sexual Exploitation: Rape, Child Sexual Abuse, and Workplace Harassment* (Beverly Hills, Calif.: Sage, 1984); Diana E. H. Russell (ed.), *Making Violence Sexy: Feminist Views on Pornography* (New York: Teachers College Press, 1993); Myra Sadker and David M. Sadker, *Failing at Fairness: How America's Schools Cheat Girls* (New York: Scribner, 1994); Peggy Reeves Sanday, *A Woman Scorned: Acquaintance Rape on Trial* (New York: Doubleday, 1996); Bernice Sandler, Lisa A. Silverberg, and Roberta M. Hall, *The Chilly Classroom Climate: A Guide to Improve the Education of Women* (Washington, D.C.: National Association for Women in Education, 1996); Marilyn Waring, *If Women Counted: A New Feminist Economics* (San Francisco: HarperCollins, 1988); Wellman, *Portraits of White Racism;* Cornel West, *Race Matters* (New York: Vintage, 1993); Naomi Wolf, *The Beauty Myth: How Images of Beauty Are Used Against Women* (New York: Morrow, 1991); James Woods, and Jay H. Lucas, *The Corporate Closet: The Professional Lives of Gay Men in America* (New York: Free Press, 1993).

4. Feagin and Sikes, *Living with Racism,* pp. 15–17.

5. Walt Harrington, "On the Road with the President of Black America," *Washington Post Magazine,* January 25, 1987, p. W14.
6. See Douglas S. Massey and Nancy A. Denton, *American Apartheid: Segregation and the Making of the Underclass* (Cambridge, Mass.: Harvard University Press, 1993).
7. Claude M. Steele, "Race and the Schooling of Black Americans," *Atlantic Monthly,* April 1992, p. 73.
8. Benjamin, *Black Elite,* p. 20; Feagin and Sikes, *Living with Racism,* p. 25.
9. Marian Wright Edelman, *The Measure of Our Success: A Letter to My Children and Yours* (Boston: Beacon Press, 1992).
10. Quoted in Feagin and Sikes, *Living with Racism,* pp. 23–24.
11. See C. Bohmer and A. Parrot, *Sexual Assault on Campus* (New York: Lexington, 1993); A. Browne and K. R. Williams, "Gender Intimacy and Legal Violence: Trends From 1976 Through 1987," *Gender and Society* 7, no. 1(1993), pp. 78–98; Center for Research on Women, *Secrets in Public;* French, *War Against Women;* Allan G. Johnson, "On the Prevalence of Rape in the United States," *Signs: Journal of Women in Culture and Society* 6, no. 1(1980), pp. 136–46; Russell, *Sexual Exploitation.*
12. See Cose, *Rage,* pp. 31, 32–33; Feagin and Sikes, *Living with Racism,* p. 213.
13. R. Roosevelt Thomas, *Beyond Race and Gender: Unleashing the Power of Your Total Work Force by Managing Diversity* (New York: AMACOM, 1991), p. 102.
14. U.S. Bureau of the Census, *Statistical Abstract of the United States, 1996* (Washington, D.C.: U.S. Government Printing Office, 1996), Table 637.
15. Ibid, Tables 649 and 739.
16. U.S. Bureau of the Census, *Money Income in the United States, 1998.* Current Population Reports Series P60-206, Table 9 (Washington, D.C.: U.S. Government Printing Office, 1999).
17. See Comstock, *Violence Against Lesbians and Gay Men;* McNaught, *Gay Issues in the Workplace;* Pharr, *Homophobia;* and Woods and Lucas, *The Corporate Closet.*
18. See Pharr, *Homophobia,* pp. 19, 23–24.
19. See Russell, *Sexual Exploitation;* Sanday, *A Woman Scorned.*
20. See Pharr, *Homophobia,* p. 26.
21. Much of this material is based on Joseph Barndt, *Dismantling Racism: The Continuing Challenge to White America* (Minneapolis: Augsburg, 1991), chapter 3; and Kivel, *Uprooting Racism,* pp. 36–58.

22. See Ruth Frankenberg, *The Social Construction of Whiteness: White Women, Race Matters* (Minneapolis: University of Minnesota Press, 1993), pp. 60–61.
23. Barndt, *Dismantling Racism,* pp. 51–52; West, *Race Matters,* p. 19.
24. See Feagin and Sikes, *Living with Racism,* p. 53.

CHAPTER 6: THE TROUBLE WITH THE TROUBLE

1. For more on this, see Richard Delgado and Jean Stefancic, "Imposition," in Richard Delgado and Jean Stefancic (eds.), *Critical White Studies: Looking Behind the Mirror* (Philadelphia: Temple University Press, 1997), pp. 98–105.
2. R. Roosevelt Thomas, *Beyond Race and Gender: Unleashing the Power of Your Total Work Force by Managing Diversity* (New York: AMACOM, 1991), p. 41.
3. Marvin Harris, *Cows, Pigs, Wars, and Witches* (New York: Random House, 1974).

CHAPTER 7: PRIVILEGE, POWER, DIFFERENCE, AND US

1. Kivel, *Uprooting Racism,* p. 83.
2. *Men Are from Mars* . . . is the title of a self-help book by John Gray, subtitled "A practical guide for improving communication and getting what you want in your relationships," published in 1992.
3. See David Thomas, "Racial Dynamics in Cross-Race Developmental Relationships," *Administrative Science Quarterly,* June 1993, pp. 169–94.

CHAPTER 8: HOW SYSTEMS OF PRIVILEGE WORK

1. For more on patriarchy and how it works, see Allan G. Johnson, *The Gender Knot: Unraveling Our Patriarchal Legacy* (Philadelphia: Temple University Press, 1997).
2. See, for example, Bernice Sandler et al., *The Chilly Classroom Climate: A Guide to Improve the Education of Women* (Washington, D.C.: National Association for Women in Education, 1996), part 4.
3. Quoted in ibid., p. 60.
4. Quoted in ibid., p. 62.
5. See Deborah Tannen, *You Just Don't Understand: Women and Men in Conversation* (New York: Morrow, 1990), and *Talking from 9 to 5* (New York: Morrow, 1994).

6. See, for example, Richard Butsch, "Class and Gender in Four Decades of Television Situation Comedy," *Critical Studies in Mass Communications* 9 (1992), pp. 387–99.
7. Feagin and Sikes, *Living with Racism,* p. 94.
8. Ibid., p. 229.
9. *America the Beautiful,* by Katharine Lee Bates, 1893.
10. For an excellent discussion of double binds, see Marilyn Frye, "Oppression," in *The Politics of Reality: Essays in Feminist Theory* (Trumansburg, N.Y.: Crossing Press, 1983).
11. For more on how this works, see Arlie Hochschild, *The Second Shift: Working Parents and the Revolution at Home* (New York: Viking/Penguin, 1989).
12. See American Association of University Women, *How Schools Shortchange Girls* (Washington, D.C.: American Association of University Women, 1992); Feagin and Sikes, *Living with Racism;* Myra Sadker and David M. Sadker, *Failing at Fairness: How America's Schools Cheat Girls* (New York: Scribner, 1994); and Sandler et al., *The Chilly Classroom Climate.*
13. See American Association of University Women, *How Schools Shortchange Girls;* and Sadker and Sadker, *Failing at Fairness.*
14. See, for example, Beverly Daniel Tatum, *Why Are All the Black Kids Sitting Together in the Cafeteria?* (New York: Basic Books, 1997).
15. Wellman, *Portraits of White Racism.*
16. Ibid., p. 222.
17. Joel Kovel, *White Racism: A Psychohistory* (New York: Pantheon, 1970), p. 212.
18. See Alexander Thomas and Samuel Sillen, *The Theory and Application of Symbolic Interactionism* (Boston: Houghton-Mifflin, 1977).

CHAPTER 9: GETTING OFF THE HOOK

1. My sources for much of this material are Kivel, *Uprooting Racism,* pp. 40–48, and Wellman, *Portraits of White Racism,* pp. 207–209.
2. Christina Hoff Sommers, "The War Against Boys," *Atlantic Monthly,* May 2000, pp. 59–74.
3. See William Ryan's classic book on this subject, *Blaming the Victim* (New York: Vintage, 1976).
4. See Douglas S. Massey and Nancy A. Denton, *American Apartheid: Segregation and the Making of the Underclass* (Cambridge, Mass.: Harvard University Press, 1993).
5. For a discussion of this, see Tatum, *Why Are All the Black Kids Sitting Together in the Cafeteria?*

6. Frankenberg, *Social Construction of Whiteness,* p. 49. Italics in original.
7. Edelman, *The Measure of Our Success.*

CHAPTER 10: WHAT CAN WE DO?

1. See Elizabeth Fisher, *Woman's Creation: Sexual Evolution and the Shaping of Society* (New York: McGraw-Hill, 1979); Gerda Lerner, *The Creation of Patriarchy* (New York: Oxford University Press, 1986).
2. This is what Warren Farrell means when he describes male power as mythical. In this case, he's right. See *The Myth of Male Power* (New York: Berkley Books, 1993).
3. J. R. Wilkie, "Changes in U.S. Men's Attitudes Towards the Family Provider Role, 1972–1989," *Gender and Society* 7, no. 2 (1993): 261–79.
4. The classic statement of how this happens is by Thomas S. Kuhn, *The Structure of Scientific Revolutions* (Chicago: University of Chicago Press, 1970).
5. Bonaro W. Overstreet, *Hands Laid Upon the Wind* (New York: Norton, 1955), p. 15.
6. For more on this, see Ward Churchill, "Crimes Against Humanity," *Z Magazine* 6 (March 1993), pp. 43–47. Reprinted in Margaret L. Andersen and Patricia Hill Collins (eds.), *Race, Class, and Gender,* 3rd ed. (Belmont, Calif.: Wadsworth, 1998), pp. 413–20.
7. William A. Gamson, "Violence and Political Power: The Meek Don't Make It," *Psychology Today* 8 (July 1974), pp. 35–41.
8. For more on this, see the excellent PBS documentary of the civil rights movement, *Eyes on the Prize.*
9. Doug McAdam, *Political Process and the Development of Black Insurgency 1930–1970* (Chicago: University of Chicago Press, 1982).
10. Frederick Douglass, Speech Before the West Indian Emancipation Society (August 4, 1857), in *The Life and Writings of Frederick Douglass,* ed. Philip S. Foner, p. 437 (New York: International Publishers, 1950).
11. See Kivel, *Uprooting Racism,* part 3, "Being Allies."
12. A lot of what follows came out of a brainstorming session with my friend and colleague Jane Tuohy as we worked out the design for a gender workshop.
13. See Suzanne Pharr, *Homophobia: A Weapon of Sexism* (Inverness, Calif.: Chardon Press, 1988).

Resources

PRIVILEGE AND OPPRESSION
ACROSS TWO OR MORE DIMENSIONS

Amott, Teresa L., and Julie A. Matthaei. *Race, Gender, and Work: A Multi-cultural Economic History of Women in the United States.* Rev. ed. Boston: South End Press, 1996.

Andersen, Margaret L., and Patricia Hill Collins, eds. *Race, Class, and Gender: An Anthology.* 3rd ed. Belmont, Calif.: Wadsworth, 1998.

Belkhir, Jean G. *An Interdisciplinary Bibliography on the Intersection of Race, Class, and Gender.* Towson, M.: Institute for Teaching and Research on Women, Towson State University, 1996. This unique bibliography is regularly updated in an electronic edition at http://www.towson.edu/~vanfoss/rgc.htm.

Collins, Patricia Hill. *Black Feminist Thought: Knowledge, Consciousness, and the Politics of Empowerment.* New York: Routledge, 1991.

Esty, Katharine, Richard Griffin, and Marcie Schorr Hirsch. *Workplace Diversity: A Manager's Guide to Solving Problems and Turning Diversity into a Competitive Advantage.* Holbrook, Mass.: Adams, 1995.

Gioseffi, Daniela, ed. *On Prejudice: A Global Perspective.* New York: Anchor Books, 1993.

Higginbotham, Elizabeth. "Black Professional Women: Job Ceilings and Employment Sectors." In *Workplace/Women's Place,* edited by Dana Dunn, pp. 234–46. Los Angeles: Roxbury, 1997.

hooks, bell. *Ain't I a Woman: Black Women and Feminism.* Boston: South End Press, 1981.

———. *Feminist Theory: From Margin to Center.* Boston: South End Press, 1984.

———. *Sisters of the Yam: Black Women and Self-Recovery.* Boston: South End Press, 1993.

———. *Talking Back: Thinking Feminism, Thinking Black.* Boston: South End Press, 1989.

Johnson, Allan G. *The Forest and the Trees: Sociology as Life, Practice, and Promise.* Philadelphia: Temple University Press, 1997.

Lerner, Gerda. "Reconceptualizing Differences Among Women." In *Feminist Frameworks.* 3rd ed., edited by Alison M. Jaggar and Paula S. Rothenberg, pp. 237–48. New York, McGraw-Hill, 1993.

Loden, Marilyn, and Judy B. Rosener. *Workforce America: Managing Employee Diversity as a Vital Resource.* Homewood, Ill.: Business One Irwin, 1991.

Lorde, Audre. *Sister Outsider: Essays and Speeches.* Freedom, Calif.: Crossing Press, 1984.

McIntosh, Peggy. "White Privilege and Male Privilege: A Personal Account of Coming to See Correspondences Through Work in Women's Studies." In *Gender Basics: Feminist Perspectives on Women and Men,* edited by Anne Minas. Belmont, Calif.: Wadsworth, 1993. This classic article is widely reprinted in anthologies.

Mills, Nicholas, ed. *Debating Affirmative Action.* New York: Dell, 1994.

Moraga, Cherríe, and Gloria Anzaldúa, eds. *This Bridge Called My Back: Writings by Radical Women of Color.* New York: Kitchen Table: Women of Color Press, 1983.

Ore, Tracy E. *The Social Construction of Difference and Inequality: Race, Class, Gender, and Sexuality.* Mountain View, Calif.: Mayfield, 2000.

Roediger, David R. *The Wages of Whiteness: Race and the Making of the American Working Class.* New York: Verso, 1991.

Rosenblum, Karen E., and Toni-Michelle C. Travis, eds. *The Meaning of Difference: American Constructions of Race, Sex and Gender, Social Class, and Sexual Orientation.* 2nd ed. New York: McGraw-Hill, 2000.

Rothenberg, Paula S., ed. *Race, Class, and Gender: An Integrated Study.* 4th ed. New York: St. Martin's, 1998.

Ryan, William. *Blaming the Victim.* New York: Vintage, 1976.

Zinn, Howard. *A People's History of the United States.* New York: Harper & Row, 1980.

GENDER PRIVILEGE AND OPPRESSION

Abramson, Joan. *Old Boys—New Women: Sexual Harassment in the Workplace.* New York: Praeger, 1993.

American Association of University Women. *How Schools Shortchange Girls.* Washington, D.C.: American Association of University Women, 1992.

Andersen, Margaret L. *Thinking about Women: Sociological Perspectives on Sex and Gender.* 5th ed. New York: Macmillan, 1999.

Benokraitis, Nijole V. "Sex Discrimination in the 21st Century." In *Subtle Sexism: Current Practice and Prospects for Change,* edited by Nijole V. Benokraitis, pp. 5–33. Thousand Oaks, Calif.: Sage, 1997.

———, and Joe R. Feagin. *Modern Sexism: Blatant, Subtle, and Covert Discrimination.* 2nd ed. Englewood Cliffs, N.J.: Prentice-Hall, 1995.

Bohmer, Carol, and Andrea Parrot. *Sexual Assault on Campus.* New York: Lexington, 1993.

Brod, Harry. "Work Clothes and Leisure Suits: The Class Basis and Bias of the Men's Movement." In *Men's Lives,* edited by Michael Kimmel and Michael A. Messner, p. 280. New York: Macmillan, 1989.

Browne, A., and K. R. Williams. "Gender Intimacy and Legal Violence: Trends From 1976 Through 1987." *Gender and Society* 7, no. 1 (1993): 78–98.

Bunch, Charlotte. "Not for Lesbians Only." *Quest* 11, no. 2 (Fall 1975).

Center for Research on Women. *Secrets in Public: Sexual Harassment in Our Schools.* Wellesley, Mass.: Wellesley College Center for Research on Women, 1993.

Chernin, Kim. *The Obsession: Reflections on the Tyranny of Slenderness.* New York: Harper & Row, 1981.

Colwill, Nina L. "Women in Management: Power and Powerlessness." In *Workplace/Women's Place,* edited by Dana Dunn, pp. 186–97. Los Angeles: Roxbury, 1997.

Corcoran-Nantes, Yvonne, and Ken Roberts. "'We've Got One of Those': The Peripheral Status of Women in Male-Dominated Industries." In *Workplace/Women's Place,* edited by Dana Dunn, pp. 271–87. Los Angeles: Roxbury, 1997.

Dunn, Dana, ed. *Workplace/Women's Place.* Los Angeles: Roxbury, 1997.

Dworkin, Andrea. *Woman Hating.* New York: Dutton, 1974.

Ehrenreich, Barbara, and Deidre English. *For Her Own Good: 150 Years of Experts' Advice to Women.* New York: Anchor Books/Doubleday, 1978.

Epstein, Cynthia Fuchs. *Deceptive Distinctions: Sex, Gender, and the Social Order.* New Haven, Conn.: Yale University Press, 1989.

Faludi, Susan. *Backlash: The Undeclared War Against American Women.* New York: Crown, 1991.

Fausto-Sterling, Anne. "The Five Sexes: Why Male and Female Are Not Enough." *Sciences* 33 (March/April 1993): 20–24.

———. *Myths of Gender: Biological Theories about Women and Men.* Rev. ed. New York: Basic Books, 1992.

Federal Glass Ceiling Commission. *A Solid Investment: Making Full Use of the Nation's Human Capital.* Washington, D.C.: Federal Glass Ceiling Commission, 1995.

French, Marilyn. *Beyond Power: On Men, Women, and Morals.* New York: Summit Books, 1985.

———. *The War Against Women.* New York: Summit Books, 1992.

Frye, Marilyn. *The Politics of Reality: Essays in Feminist Theory.* Trumansburg, N.Y.: Crossing Press, 1983.

Gardner, Carol Brooks. *Passing By: Gender and Public Harassment.* Berkeley: University of California Press, 1995.

Haslett, Beth Bonniwell, and Susan Lipman. "Micro Inequities: Up Close and Personal." *Subtle Sexism: Current Practice and Prospects for Change,* edited by Nijole V. Benokraitis, pp. 34–53. Thousand Oaks, Calif.: Sage, 1997.

Helgesen, Sally. "Women's Ways of Leading." In Dunn, Dana (ed.). *Workplace/Women's Place*, edited by Dana Dunn, pp. 181–85. Los Angeles: Roxbury, 1997.

Hochschild, Arlie. *The Second Shift: Working Parents and the Revolution at Home*. New York: Viking/Penguin, 1989.

Hosken, Fran P. *The Hosken Report: Genital and Sexual Mutilation of Females*. 4th rev. ed. Lexington, Mass.: Women's International Network News, 1994.

Johnson, Allan G. *The Gender Knot: Unraveling Our Patriarchal Legacy*. Philadelphia: Temple University Press, 1997.

———. "On the Prevalence of Rape in the United States." *Signs: Journal of Women in Culture and Society* 6, no. 1(1980).

Kaufman, Michael, ed. *Beyond Patriarchy*. New York: Oxford, 1987.

Kimmel, Michael. *Manhood in America: A Cultural History*. New York: Free Press, 1996.

———, and Michael Messner, eds. *Men's Lives*. 4th ed. Boston: Allyn & Bacon, 1997.

Lederer, Laura, ed. *Take Back the Night: Women on Pornography*. New York: Morrow, 1980.

Loden, Marilyn. *Feminine Leadership*. New York: Random House, 1985.

Lorber, Judith. *Paradoxes of Gender*. New Haven, Conn.: Yale University Press, 1995.

MacKinnon, Catharine A. *Only Words*. Cambridge, Mass.: Harvard University Press, 1993.

Moore, Lynda L. *Not As Far As You Think: The Realities of Working Women*. Lexington, Mass.: Lexington Books, 1986.

Morgan, Robin, ed. *Sisterhood Is Global: The International Women's Movement Anthology*. New York: Anchor Books, 1984.

Paludi, Michele A. *Ivory Power: Sexual Harassment on Campus*. Albany: State University of New York Press, 1990.

Pharr, Suzanne. *Homophobia: A Weapon of Sexism*. Inverness, Calif.: Chardon Press, 1988.

Reardon, Kathleen Kelley. "Dysfunctional Communication Patterns in the Workplace: Closing the Gap Between Women and Men." In *Workplace/Women's Place*, edited by Dana Dunn, pp. 165–80. Los Angeles: Roxbury, 1997.

———. *They Don't Get It, Do They?* Boston: Little, Brown, 1995.

Rhode, Deborah L. *Speaking of Sex: The Denial of Gender Inequality*. Cambridge, Mass.: Harvard University Press, 1997.

Rich, Adrienne. *Of Woman Born*. New York: Norton, 1976.

Rosenberg, Janet, Harry Perlstadt, and William R. F. Phillips. "'Now that We Are Here': Discrimination, Disparagement, and Harassment at Work and the Experience of Women Lawyers." In *Workplace/*

Women's Place, edited by Dana Dunn, pp. 247–59. Los Angeles: Roxbury, 1997.

Rotundo, Anthony. *American Manhood: Transformations in Masculinity from the Revolution to the Modern Era.* New York: Basic Books, 1993.

Russell, Diana E. H. *Sexual Exploitation: Rape, Child Sexual Abuse, and Workplace Harassment.* Beverly Hills, Calif.: Sage, 1984.

———, ed. *Making Violence Sexy: Feminist Views on Pornography.* New York: Teachers College Press, 1993.

Sadker, Myra, and David M. Sadker. *Failing at Fairness: How America's Schools Cheat Girls.* New York: Scribner, 1994.

Sanday, Peggy Reeves. *A Woman Scorned: Acquaintance Rape on Trial.* New York: Doubleday, 1996.

Sandler, Bernice, Lisa A. Silverberg, and Roberta M. Hall. *The Chilly Classroom Climate: A Guide to Improve the Education of Women.* Washington, D.C.: National Association for Women in Education, 1996.

Schultz, Vicki. "Reconceptualizing Sexual Harassment." *Yale Law Journal,* April 1998, pp. 1683–1805.

Swerdlow, Marian. "Men's Accommodations to Women Entering a Nontraditional Occupation: A Case of Rapid Transit Operatives." In *Workplace/Women's Place,* edited by Dana Dunn, pp. 260–70. Los Angeles: Roxbury, 1997.

Tannen, Deborah. *Talking from 9 to 5.* New York: Morrow, 1994.

———. *You Just Don't Understand: Women and Men in Conversation.* New York: Morrow, 1990.

Thorne, Barrie. *Gender Play: Girls and Boys in School.* New Brunswick, N.J.: Rutgers University Press, 1993.

Waring, Marilyn. *If Women Counted: A New Feminist Economics.* San Francisco: HarperCollins, 1988.

Wilkie, J. R. "Changes in U.S. Men's Attitudes Towards the Family Provider Role, 1972–1989." *Gender and Society* 7, no. 2 (1993): 261–79.

Williams, Christine L. *Still a Man's World: Men Who Do Women's Work.* Berkeley: University of California Press, 1995.

Wolf, Naomi. *The Beauty Myth: How Images of Beauty Are Used Against Women.* New York: Morrow, 1991.

RACE PRIVILEGE AND OPPRESSION

Allen, Theodore W. *The Invention of the White Race: Racial Oppression and Social Control,* vol. 1-2. New York: Verso, 1994, 1997.

Allport, Gordon W. *The Nature of Prejudice.* New York: Anchor, 1958.

Baldwin, James. "On Being 'White'. . . and Other Lies." *Essence* 14 (April 1984): 90–92.

Barndt, Joseph. *Dismantling Racism: The Continuing Challenge to White America.* Minneapolis: Augsburg, 1991.

Bell, Derrick. *And We Are Not Saved: The Elusive Quest for Racial Justice.* New York: Basic Books, 1987.

———. *Faces at the Bottom of the Well: The Permanence of Racism.* New York: Basic Books, 1992.

Benjamin, Lois. *The Black Elite: Facing the Color Line in the Twilight of the Twentieth Century.* Chicago: Nelson-Hall, 1991.

Churchill, Ward. "Crimes Against Humanity." *Z Magazine* 6 (March 1993): 43–47. Reprinted in Margaret L. Andersen and Patricia Hill Collins, eds., *Race, Class, and Gender.* 3rd ed., pp. 413–20. Belmont, Calif.: Wadsworth, 1998.

Collins, Patricia Hill. *Black Feminist Thought: Knowledge, Consciousness, and the Politics of Empowerment.* New York: Routledge, 1991.

Cose, Ellis. *The Rage of a Privileged Class.* New York: HarperCollins, 1993.

Davis, Angela Y. *Women, Race, and Class.* New York: Random House, 1981.

Delgado, Richard, and Jean Stefancic, eds. *Critical White Studies.* Philadelphia: Temple University Press, 1997.

Dovidio, John F., and Samuel L. Gaertner, eds. *Prejudice, Discrimination, and Racism.* Orlando, Fla.: Academic Press, 1986.

Edelman, Marian Wright. *The Measure of Our Success: A Letter to My Children and Yours.* Boston: Beacon Press, 1992.

Feagin, Joe R., and Melvin P. Sikes. *Living with Racism: The Black Middle-Class Experience.* Boston: Beacon Press, 1994.

Frankenberg, Ruth. *The Social Construction of Whiteness: White Women, Race Matters.* Minneapolis: University of Minnesota Press, 1993.

Hacker, Andrew. *Two Nations: Black and White, Separate, Hostile, Unequal.* New York: Scribner, 1992.

Kivel, Paul. *Uprooting Racism: How White People Can Work for Racial Justice.* Philadelphia: New Society Publishers, 1996.

Kovel, Joel. *White Racism: A Psychohistory.* New York: Pantheon, 1970.

Massey, Douglas S., and Nancy A. Denton. *American Apartheid: Segregation and the Making of the Underclass.* Cambridge, Mass.: Harvard University Press, 1993.

Steele, Claude M. "Race and the Schooling of Black Americans." *Atlantic Monthly,* April 1992, p. 73.

Takaki, Ronald. *Strangers from a Different Shore: A History of Asian-Americans.* Boston: Little, Brown, 1989.

Tatum, Beverly Daniel. *Why Are All the Black Kids Sitting Together in the Cafeteria?* New York: Basic Books, 1997.

Terry, Robert. "The Negative Impact on White Values." In Benjamin P. Bowser and Raymond Hunt, eds., *Impacts of Racism on White Americans.* Newbury Park, Calif.: Sage, 1981.

Thomas, Roosevelt R. *Beyond Race and Gender: Unleashing the Power of Your Total Work Force by Managing Diversity.* New York: AMACOM, 1991.

Thomas, David. "Racial Dynamics in Cross-Race Developmental Relationships." *Administrative Science Quarterly* (June 1993): 169–94.

Thomas, Alexander, and Samuel Sillen. *Racism and Psychiatry.* New York: Brunner/Mazel, 1972.

Wellman, David T. *Portraits of White Racism.* 2nd ed. New York: Cambridge University Press, 1993.

West, Cornel. *Race Matters.* New York: Vintage, 1993.

PRIVILEGE, OPPRESSION, AND SEXUAL ORIENTATION

Abelove, Henry, Michele Aina Barale, and David M. Halperin, eds. *The Lesbian and Gay Studies Reader.* New York: Routledge, 1993.

Baker, Dan, and Sean Strub. *Cracking the Corporate Closet.* New York: HarperCollins, 1993.

Comstock, David Gary. *Violence Against Lesbians and Gay Men.* New York: Columbia University Press, 1991.

McNaught, Brian. *Gay Issues in the Workplace.* New York: St. Martin's, 1993.

Miller, Neil. *Out of the Past: Gay and Lesbian History from 1869 to the Present.* New York: Vintage, 1995.

Pharr, Suzanne. *Homophobia: A Weapon of Sexism.* Inverness, Calif: Chardon Press, 1988.

Woods, James, and Jay H. Lucas. *The Corporate Closet: The Professional Lives of Gay Men in America.* New York: Free Press, 1993.

SOCIAL CLASS PRIVILEGE AND OPPRESSION

Danziger, Sheldon, and Peter Gottschalk. *Uneven Tides: Rising Inequality in America.* New York: Russell Sage Foundation, 1993.

Ehrenreich, Barbara. *Fear of Falling: The Inner Life of the Middle Class.* New York: HarperCollins, 1989.

Gilbert, Dennis, and Joseph A. Kahl. *The American Class Structure: A New Synthesis.* 5th ed. Belmont, Calif.: Wadsworth, 1997.

Kerbo, Harold R. *Social Stratification and Inequality.* 4th ed. New York: McGraw-Hill, 1999.

Schor, Juliet B. *The Overworked American: The Unexpected Decline of Leisure.* New York: Basic Books, 1993.

Sennett, Richard, and Jonathan Cobb. *The Hidden Injuries of Class.* New York: Vintage, 1973.

Index